How To ▌ A Non-Den▐ al Wedding Ceremony:
Everything You Need To Know To Create And Officiate A Personalized Wedding For Friends And Family

J.P. Reynolds, M.Div.

D0652506

Copyright © 2017 by J.P. Reynolds
All rights reserved
ISBN: 9781521270714

Here's what some of the Wedding Industry's top pros have to say about JP Reynolds and his approach to creating memorable wedding ceremonies!

Finding an officiant is one of the most important parts of a wedding ceremony. It is, after all, the person who pronounces a couple's "happily ever after." Personalized, unique, romantic – these are the attributes that make JP Reynolds one of Southern California's most sought-after officiants. Now he shares his years of marital wit and wisdom – and we're talking a thousand marriages under his belt – with you, the loved one who has been asked to conduct a ceremony. Flattered, you said "yes" – and now you're completely stressed out! This expertly written guide will help you craft the perfect ceremony, from the basic flow to tips on vows, blessings and more without repeating the same words heard round the marital world. After conducting countless nuptials, JP has crafted a unique, but simple structure that results in a ceremony filled with love, laughter, beauty and romance.

Lara Morgenson Burnap, Editor-in-Chief, California Wedding Day Magazine

There is something special about JP. His ceremonies somehow bring you closer to the couple, as a witness, as he finds a way to bring out the most precious nuances of their love and their bond. So many ceremonies feel rehearsed or rote, however JP's are memorable, thoughtful, reflective and embrace the heart of the reason for the ritual, allowing us to all hear the words as though hearing them for the very first time.

Kristin Banta, Principal Designer and CEO of Kristin Banta Events, Inc.

JP Reynolds has the most unique approach to weddings and truly grasps each couple's vision so as to make a treasured memory for their lifetime together. He brings fresh light to each ceremony he conducts by incorporating each couple's personalities and style so that no two ceremonies are alike. His years of experience show through his confidence in front of any audience, large or small, and through the variety of beliefs and lifestyles he works with. This book will inspire you to conduct ceremonies with grace, uniqueness and most important of all, with love.

Patty Bell, Associate Director of Sales and Catering, The Ranch, Laguna Beach

JP is a true professional. If you want to take advice from anyone about how to devise the perfect wedding ceremony, he is your guy! Weddings are so personal and each couple is truly unique. JP really focuses in on that and tailors each of his weddings to show the spirit, love and strength of the couple's relationship. Not only are there tear-jerking moments in his ceremonies, but he also uses a bit of humor to keep you captivated. Now take all of his advice, sprinkle in some of your own personal touches and personality and you will have the perfect wedding ceremony!

Brooke Keegan, Founder Brooke Keegan Special Events & Design Studio

In dealing with clients from a wide variety of religious, cultural and ethnic backgrounds, JP provides the one thing that I really need – the ability to guide ceremonies that are non-denominational but still retain the values, meaning and sensitivity that the wedding day must exemplify. Having a family member or close friend officiate brings a much deeper meaning to the wedding ceremony. But if you are unprepared it can be a disaster. Follow the guidance JP lays out in this book and you will be able to give your couple the most special of wedding gifts – a ceremony they will remember forever!

Jeannie Savage, Founder and President of Details, Details Wedding and Event Planning

What I look for in an officiant for my clients is someone who wants to 'get' them. Someone who takes the time to find out who they are, where they've been and where they're going in life. For it is armed with that knowledge that the officiant will craft a ceremony that is the most meaningful for the couple and everyone at the wedding. I've just described JP. He has the interest, the heart and the presence to be one of the best officiants around. I never do a wedding with JP when I don't hear the guests say, "what an incredibly beautiful, moving and meaningful ceremony!" Guest officiants who use this book will learn how to gift their loved ones with a warm and inspiring ceremony.

Paula Laskelle, Founder of Champagne Taste Wedding Design

Now join your hands,

and with your hands

your hearts.

Shakespeare

TABLE OF CONTENTS

NEW Bonus Sections!

INTRODUCTION

Congratulations! To officiate a wedding ceremony, especially for a couple you know and love, is truly one of life's great honors and delights.

I presume that when your couple invited you to conduct their ceremony you felt surprised, flattered and excited. Then, a little later, chances are you began to wonder –What did I get myself into? How do I conduct a wedding ceremony?!

Well, I've written this book as an answer to your question, "Now what do I do?"

As a non-denominational wedding officiant, I've celebrated over one-thousand ceremonies during the past twenty years. I've worked with couples ranging from their early twenties through their eighties. I've helped couples say their "I Do's" from The Ritz to grandma's backyard. And eight of those weddings were featured on reality TV programs – hey, I live in Los Angeles!

I'm also a corporate communications coach and much of my work is about showing business professionals how to speak and present with confidence.

I love celebrating weddings and I'm happy that your couple has honored you with the request of being their officiant. For you to say, "I now pronounce you married" will mean more to your couple than you can imagine.

I've written this book to help you understand what a ceremony is all about so you can craft a ceremony that is personalized for your couple. **This is a guide and not a script**. Your couple asked you to perform their ceremony because they don't want it canned or stilted. They want something fresh and not something that just mimics a church service.

This book shows you how to craft and word a ceremony that reflects your couple AND showcases your style and personality. While couples will find this book helpful as they think about what they want their ceremony to look and feel like, I specifically want to work with you, their chosen officiant.

Whether you and the couple together create the ceremony or they ask you to take charge, the most important thing is that the ceremony reflects the taste, style and belief of the couple. And while whatever they want is fine, oftentimes, a couple doesn't know exactly what it is they want.

Part of your job is to help them explain what it is they want for their ceremony and then craft a ceremony that, in form and tone, gives them what they envisioned. You also want the ceremony to inspire and refresh their family and friends.

A tall order? Yes. Doable? Very much so!

This book is made up of Three Parts:

Part One: I share with you my philosophy about weddings and how that influences the way I craft a ceremony.

Part Two: I take you through each of the various moments in a ceremony and show you how to organize the ceremony so that it has flow and energy – so that it is romantic without being cheesy!

Part Three: I offer you tips and techniques for how to speak with confidence during the ceremony, so you can inspire all present and maybe even get folks teary-eyed. Hey, it's a wedding so let those handkerchiefs wave!

Bonus Sections: I give you selections of vows, blessings, "non-blessings" and inspirational sayings, along with checklists, readings, and wordings for introducing each segment of the ceremony.

New Bonus Sections: This Revised Edition includes interviews with first-time officiants who share their perspectives on the experience. I also share with you a "before and after" ceremony script from a first time officiant I coached.

Your couple invited you to officiate their ceremony because they want something that is uniquely theirs and not clichéd drivel from some unknown officiant. The ceremony is your gift to the couple and I'm going to show you how to give them a gift that will be a touchstone for their life together.

PART 1

WHAT IS A WEDDING?

No matter if the wedding takes place at a 5-star resort or under a tree at a neighborhood park; no matter if there are two guests or two hundred, every wedding does three things:

Gives thanks for the past
Celebrates the present
Honors the future

And every wedding does all this in the most human of ways – with a couple's family and friends eating, drinking and making merry; telling stories that are sweet, wonderful and maybe even just plain outrageous; and most especially by embracing the couple with hopes and wishes.

It is that simple and that profound.

Couples often tell me they can't wait to start their life together. The truth is their life together began the moment they first met – in a classroom, at a crowded bar, or with the click of the "send" button at an on-line dating site.

A couple's wedding is their pledge to honor that meeting and all the meetings that came after. To honor all the good that it has made of them and all the good that it will make of them all the days of their life together.

A couple's wedding affirms and seals that life with the giving of their word: "I Do promise to continue to become the best and bravest person I am meant to be.

I Do promise to support and cheer on my partner as he, as she, becomes the best and bravest person they are meant to be."

A wedding ceremony is an affirmation of who the couple is at this moment in time and of who they want to become.

true story ~

The reception was in full swing as couples took to the dance floor for YMCA. After a few get-down-and-party tunes, the DJ switched over to a "slow dance." Within moments, there was just one couple on the dance floor. They were in their late 70's. He was dapper; she was stylish. I vividly recall how utterly charmed I was by the sight of them dancing.

They were fluid, deft, and sensual. Yes, sensual. In fact, I thought they were more sensual than any couple I had seen that evening (except, of course, for the bride and groom). They were two people dancing as one.

I saw this couple a year later. Another wedding. Another reception. And again, I was utterly taken by the sight of them on the dance floor. Yes, they knew how to dance; but, it was more than that. I don't know how to describe them other than to say that they shined with an intimacy seldom revealed by a couple in public.

At the second reception I decided to tell them how beautiful I thought they looked – they were my new rock star couple. And I wanted to know their secret – how did they learn to dance with such ease and grace?

They were surprised and tickled that they had such an affect on me. Their "secret," though, took me by surprise as it was so simple.

They told me that they've always been interested in each other. Interested in what the other was thinking and feeling and doing. The woman said, "For forty-three years we've been each other's eyes." And, yes, her eyes sparkled when she told me that.

During their wedding ceremony, many couples will have a candle lighting ritual, a.k.a. "The Unity Candle." There are variations on the theme of this candle. Essentially, though, each takes a lit taper and together light a large candle that rests between the tapers. By way of introducing this ritual, I read the following – a reflection from a mystic:

From every human being there rises a light that reaches straight to heaven. And when two souls that are destined to be together find each other, their streams of light flow together and a single, brighter light goes forth from their united being.

I love the intensity of the imagery. Traditionally, the couple blows out their tapers. However, I urge them to keep their tapers lit, as I don't believe a person's "light" is extinguished through the blending of lights. It is simply a myth that "two become one." In marriage, two people come together, challenge and protect each other so that each can become the best and bravest that they are meant to be. And they do all this in the light of the other.

I think this was the reality of that couple whose dancing remains with me to this day. They were two people whose individual "lights" blended in such a way on that dance floor that they lit up the room – lit up the night, as their own light shone upon each other.

I believe a wedding celebrates what already exists. A couple invites family and friends and asks them to celebrate the great good they have found in each other and to bear witness as they pledge their life to each other.

A wedding is a wonderful gift a couple gives to family and friends. Folks can put aside the messiness of daily life and focus on what really matters – love, loyalty and friendship.

I believe the job of an officiant is to help the couple, their families and friends remember that this is what their celebration is all about. This now is your job!

PART 2

HOW TO CRAFT A WEDDING CEREMONY

People often think that if they're not having a religious ceremony, then they're left with a vaguely imagined "civil" ceremony. However, there is a third alternative and that's a ceremony that honors the couple's life in a way that's warm, personal and has meaningful ritual.

When creating the couple's ceremony, keep in mind that people go to a wedding ceremony not expecting much. They hope it won't be too long, too boring or too depressing – we've all sat through those "marriage is hard work" sermons! Most guests have heard the clichés and seen "Wedding Crashers" and "Bridesmaids."

Also, in our daily lives, most of us are not used to hearing someone speak in a warm, intelligent and engaging way. We go to work and are bored to distraction with mind-numbing PowerPoint presentations. And for those of us who go to a church or synagogue we often have to tune out pious claptrap that we've listened to for decades on end.

People presume they'll have fun at the reception, but the ceremony? Well that's another story altogether. Expectations are low.

I presume that your couple has asked you to officiate because you know and love them. However, just because you know and love the couple doesn't mean you automatically will be more engaging and fun than a minister, judge or Elvis impersonator!

Remember These Three Core Truths:

CORE TRUTH #1: People's attention span is VERY limited. That 20-25 minute mark is ideal for a ceremony – beginning from when you take your place until the time the couple has their mad, passionate Hollywood kiss.

More is not always better, but I've found that 10 minutes is too short – guests feel gipped and wonder why the couple even bothered to have a ceremony. Longer than 25 minutes and you need Cirque du Soleil to perform!

CORE TRUTH #2: A wedding is NOT the time and place for an officiant to deliver a lecture on "what is a marriage." If the couple doesn't know what marriage is about, then it's a little late for the Power Point presentation! Trust me – no one goes to a wedding ceremony hoping to gain insight into the existential meaning of marriage.

Five years after the wedding, no one is going to remember what you said, not even you. But, five years later people will remember the tone and feel of the ceremony and they'll either smile or grunt.

A wedding ceremony, when done well, should leave people feeling refreshed. They head off into the reception excited to celebrate – despite all the challenges life might be throwing their way.

CORE TRUTH #3: You, as the officiant, are the host of the ceremony – not the center of it. You're the person who has the responsibility and power to tap into the emotional core of the experience. You are the voice for all present.

What's often forgotten is that the officiant is not the one who "marries" the couple. The bride and groom "marry" themselves. From the local government, usually the County, they purchase a license and, in front of you and all present, they verbally enter into a legal agreement. You are the official witness for the government. Not very romantic, I know! How that agreement is celebrated and understood is up to the couple.

The ceremony is the heart and soul of what basically is a legal procedure. It is your responsibility to bring all the emotional "stuff" to the surface and to make sure that the couple feels all the love and affection that family and friends heap upon them that day.

While you're the official witness, all present are witnesses. All have helped bring the couple to this moment in time. And if it's a ceremony done in the presence of God, then all there are the living embodiment of God's blessings.

Keep these three core truths in mind and you'll be able to create a ceremony that people will remember for all the right reasons!

A WEDDING CEREMONY HAS 3 KEY ELEMENTS

Structure
Content
Presentation

STRUCTURE

Keep it simple!

The heart of the ceremony is the exchange of vows and exchange of rings.

Everything prior is a prelude to the vows + rings and everything after is what I call "icing on the cake," rituals that add texture.

The ceremony should have a beginning, middle and end with a continuous flow throughout. No one moment should stop the ceremony dead in its tracks. This means there should be no long readings (or too many readings – more than two is pushing it) and no long lectures on the meaning and purpose of marriage. Nor do you want to turn the ceremony into a concert by having somebody sing and everybody just stares at the couple while listening. Music should be used in the body of the ceremony to accompany some other action (like a unity ritual or a ritual honoring families). Only if the singer is a true professional should you consider letting someone sing in a stand-alone moment.

You want the ceremony to have FLOW! You want to keep the focus on the couple. The longest section of the ceremony should be The Exchange of Vows and The Exchange of Rings.

Avoid cluttering up the ceremony with "stuff" just for the sake of filling time and space. Everything should be in service of highlighting the couple.

No matter how traditional or contemporary or off-beat a couple's style, their ceremony will contain some, most or all of the following moments, completely dependent upon their tastes and wishes:

Processional

Presentation Of The Bride

Words Of Welcome

Opening Prayer

Reading

Words Of Good Cheer From The Officiant

Exchange Of Vows

Exchange Of Rings

Unity Ritual

Honoring Of Families

Blessing / Sending Forth

Pronouncement And Presentation Of The Couple

Kiss

Recessional

As we look at each of these distinct moments, I'll explain what each is and suggest options and ways in which to personalize them to your couple.

The only two elements needed for a wedding are: the Exchange Of Vows and the Pronouncement of Marriage. Everything else is optional.

CONTENT

If you check with any of the books that offer sample ceremony scripts, you'll see that there are various ways to order the ceremony. I prefer to have an order of service that has a logical flow to it – at least by my standards of logic! Everything here is simply my preference; use it however you like as you make it work for you and the couple.

Processional

This is the order in which members of the wedding party, i.e. honored family (parents, grandparents), you, the groom, the wedding party (i.e. groomsmen, bridesmaids, ring bearer, flower girls), and the bride and her escort walk to assigned places / seats.

The venue's wedding coordinator or the coordinator hired by the couple conducts the rehearsal and works with the couple to arrange the Order of Procession. If there is no coordinator, then the couple must recruit a trusted friend to act as what I call "traffic coordinator" for the ceremony. This is the person who, at the appropriate time, will invite guests to take their seats (groomsmen usually help with this task) and will line up those who will be processing down the aisle (or equivalent).

You cannot do this job because you are the officiant, not the coordinator! Besides, you are in the wedding party procession. If the couple chooses not to hire a coordinator, then they MUST turn to a friend or family member who has strong organizational skills and is reliable.

I typically leave the logistics of the Processional to the coordinator. Most times, though, I lead the groom and his groomsmen (or in some cases grooms-women) to our place.

While there's a traditional order to the procession, the realities of modern day families have turned this into a ceremony moment that can have potential for sensitive politics. As the officiant, you need to be aware of drama and politics!

During a recent meeting with a couple, I asked the bride if she wanted to be escorted down the aisle by just her father or her father and mother (a popular option). She quickly glanced at her fiancé and hesitated in such a way that I knew something was up. Turns out, she and her parents are in a strained period of their relationship. And while her parents are going to attend the wedding, there's not a lot of warm, fuzzy love going round. The bride asked if she could just walk down the aisle alone.

Basically, she and her fiancé can do whatever they want – this is their wedding. However, my experience has been that no matter the length of the aisle it is an ENORMOUS walk for any bride to do alone.

And so we came up with an easy, elegant solution. The groom's parents would walk down first, followed by the bride's parents. The groom would stand on the aisle at the top last row and wait for the bride as she makes the walk, on her own, from the back holding room. Then, together, they'd walk down the aisle.

Given that they're paying for the wedding and have been together almost five years, there is a symbolic logic to their walking together at the beginning of the ceremony.

Different? Yes, this is not traditional. However, this solves the bride's challenge of how to tell her father that she doesn't want him to walk her down the aisle. More importantly, the bride honors her feelings and she and her fiancé have a ceremony that speaks to their integrity as a couple.

Welcome to the wacky world of wedding politics! While the politics does not directly affect you in your role as officiant, you need to be alert to the emotional under-currents swirling about the wedding, so you don't inadvertently say or do the wrong thing.

Note: When everyone in the wedding party has processed down the aisle, usually the music ends and then the bride's entrance music begins. When her music starts, you want to invite all to stand. You can do this either by actually saying, "Please stand" or by raising your hands upwards.

Presentation Of The Bride:

When the bride and her escort (traditionally her father) reach the end of the aisle, the music fades and then you have two options:

Option #1. The most traditional thing is for the officiant to ask: "Who presents this woman to this man in marriage?" Depending on who has escorted her, the answer could be, "I do" or "her mother and I" or "her family and I."

Note: You're not asking, "Who gives away this woman?" which is the old wording when a woman was her father's possession.

Often times the bride wants the question asked as it is a nod to tradition and many fathers have looked forward to the day when this question would be asked of them.

However, the escort alone does not have to answer the question. For instance, if the bride's birth parents are divorced, remarried, and all get along, then sometimes all four "parental units" say in unison, "We do!"

Sometimes, the bride wants both her parents to escort her, but her mother is not comfortable with the idea. The bride, though, wants to incorporate her mother right from the beginning and so, when she and her father reach the end of the aisle, as the music fades, the bride's mother takes a step over to her daughter's side and then, when I ask the question, both parents say, "We do."

However it plays out, once you've asked the question and the escort responds, then you tap the groom, who has been standing by your side, and he goes and shakes hands with the escort. Then together the bride and groom take their place in front of you (traditionally). The escort(s) takes a seat.

Option #2. The question does not need to be asked. In this scenario, the bride and her escort reach the end of the aisle, the music fades, you tap the groom, who has been standing by your side, and he goes and shakes hands with the escort and then the bride and groom take their place in front of you (traditionally). The escort(s) takes a seat.

Note: Make sure the Maid Of Honor takes the bride's bouquet so the bride is free to hold both hands with the groom. If there is no Maid Of Honor, then you should take the bouquet and hand it to someone in the front row (pre-selected).

Words of Welcome:

This is where you'll often hear the classic words:

> *Dearly Beloved, we are gathered here today in the presence of these witnesses, to join _____ and _____ in matrimony, which is commended to be honorable among all men; and therefore is not by any to be entered into unadvisedly or lightly – but reverently, discreetly, advisedly and solemnly BLAH, BLAH, BLAH!*

Hit the snooze button! Nothing kills the joy of a ceremony faster than clichés recited in a bland or sanctimonious tone of voice. Unless the couple wants the traditional wording, don't go there.

Your first words should be ones of welcome on behalf of the bride and groom. This only makes sense since you are the "host" of the ceremony.

Next, introduce yourself. Explain your relationship to the couple. Let everyone know that you are honored and thrilled to speak on behalf of all present (and for all who could not be present). While you don't want to do stand-up, establishing a light-hearted tone is great to do at the beginning.

The couple is nervous. Trust me. It is an out-of-body experience for them. And so I usually invite them to turn around (if they're facing me) and look out at their guests and simply soak in all the love. This breaks the ice. It helps the couple situate themselves. Guests usually smile, laugh, wave or blow kisses. They suddenly realize they're a part of all this and it's not going to be a by-the-book, stuffy affair.

I then invite family and friends to look around and recognize just how remarkable they are. In a world gone mad, they are a gathering of love. This is also an appropriate time to recall the abiding love of those who are deceased, if the couple wants to honor the memory of any loved ones.

There are various ways in which you can honor the deceased. The simplest is to acknowledge their abiding love. I say, "And it's good, too, to recall that laced through our celebration is the abiding love of____" and I mention the loved ones by name. If there are too many people, then I refer to them by their relationship to the couple, i.e. "Jill's grandparents, John's aunts", etc.

Another way to honor the deceased is to have an empty seat in the front row on which is a flower, a photo and/or a bible.

The mother of one of my bride's died a few months before the wedding and so the bride asked me to mention in my opening words the various aspects of the wedding that her mom had helped her plan.

The main thing is that a remembering of deceased loved ones not turn into a memorial service or cast a shadow over the joy.

Once "welcome" has been made and the tone set, you can do anything you want!

Opening Prayer

If the couple wants to bring a strong spiritual dimension to the ceremony, then an Opening Prayer can be offered – by you or by a relative or friend with a special connection to the couple.

This is a prayer of thanksgiving for the couple and the gift of their love in the lives of all present. It is an asking of God to bless not only the couple in their life together, but also asking God to bless all who rejoice in the couple's love and life. (See Bonus Section for samples of Opening Prayers).

Reading

Sometimes a couple wants to have a reading. The passage from St. Paul's Letter To The Corinthians, "love is patient, love is kind" is the all-time wedding fav and has been skewered in the movies and usually has guests roll their eyes (harsh, but true).

A reading serves two purposes:

First, it puts the brakes on the ceremony and lets a couple catch their breath and say to themselves, "OMG we're really here!" The couple will not hear the reading. I look into people's eyes and I know they have no idea what's being read. I'm convinced you could read from the phone book and couples would still smile and get teary-eyed!

Second, a reading serves a "political" purpose. If there are one or more people who the couple wants to honor and put the spotlight on and they're not sure how, this is an excellent way in which to do so.

A reading should be "short." Attention span is limited. How we understand a passage while reading it and how we take it in while listening to it read aloud are two different processes. It's harder to absorb a long reading while listening than it is while reading it. Distractions are everywhere, especially if you're outdoors.

Also, weddings are a very emotional time. There are people there who changed the diapers of the bride or groom, who watched them grow up, who partied with them and/or who partied with them and have been paid off not to tell they've partied with them!

There are people there who have been happily married for years, while others may be "stuck" in an unhappy relationship. Single guests may wonder if they'll ever have what the couple has found.

Emotions abound. People are not super focused on the reading. However, they do pay attention to who does the reading. The couple should invite someone(s) who has meaning in their life. The power of the reading is not simply in the words. The power comes from the emotional impact of that particular person(s) giving the reading.

Ways to do a reading:

1. One person could give the reading OR two people could do the reading, alternating stanzas. It could be a married couple whose life the couple admires. It could be siblings not in the wedding party or children of the couple. It could be the Best Man and the Maid Of Honor.

2. If it is a more intimate gathering, I've had the couple select a reading of ten or more lines and then divide it into two line segments. Five people are assigned a segment and they read it like a wave at a football game. These readers are seated in various places, and when I introduce the reading, the first person stands, reads their lines, sits down, the next person pops up and reads their lines, then the third person, etc. until the reading is completed. This makes the reading dynamic and involves more people. Also, it feels like the reading is coming forth from the guests and has the feel of a community blessing or wishing.

3. One couple decided they each would select a reading, but not show their choice to the other. The reading was a "gift" to each other. This was a fun idea in that they really did pay attention since they were curious as to what the other had selected. The readers were instructed not to show their selection, even if bribed! It was a personal touch done in a light-handed manner.

Another couple liked this idea and took it a step further – they read their own selections to each other.

4. If a couple selects two readings, they should not be read back-to-back. People will tune out that second reading, as they don't have enough attention power to listen. That second reading (the shorter of the two) should be placed later in the ceremony. I usually have the 2nd Reading take place right before the Final Blessing or Sending Forth.

Some couples want three and even four readings in the ceremony. I advise against having more than two readings. No matter how beautiful the sentiments, guests can't absorb that many readings – unless they are a literary or theatrical bunch! I suggest that the couple include the third reading in the printed Program.

If English is not the first language of either the bride or groom, or of their parents, then a reading is a great place where you can honor their language and culture. You can have the reading offered first in the mother tongue and then immediately read in English (by the same or a different person). The mother tongue should go first – out of respect.

How to introduce the reading: I simply say, "Jill and Jack have invited Jill's Aunt Polly to gift us with a reading" or some such depending on how the reading will be done.

Keep the intro short and no need to explain what the reading is about, unless there's a cute explanation as to why the reading was chosen.

Words Of "Good Cheer" From The Officiant

In a religious setting, this is where the minister, rabbi or priest would offer a "sermon" on "what is a marriage." Sadly, it's not uncommon for the religious celebrant to throw a wet blanket on the proceedings by offering words that are abstract, irrelevant or plain old depressing!

So often, the officiant, even if not a religiously ordained minister, feels compelled to "preach." He or she will talk in lofty terms about the duties of marriage or the benefits of marriage or the trials of marriage. They lecture. And it all seems like a Mad Libs game, where you fill in the blanks with the clichés of "marriage is _____" or "in life, there will be _____" or "remember that you must _____ because your vows will _____."

Although these officiants are well intentioned, what they say just goes in one ear and out the other. It doesn't stick. Their words do not encourage or inspire people. They speak in abstract terms and as people we are not geared to remember abstractions.

What we remember and what most moves our hearts is a good story – a story based in a vivid image.

A wedding is a day for wishing and hoping and you are in a unique position because you are the voice of all present. Rather than offering the usual script, gift the couple with a wish that you offer on behalf of everyone.

The couple has asked you to officiate their wedding because they want their ceremony to be personal. This is the moment in the ceremony when YOU can most personalize it.

I encourage you to think of a story or an image that speaks to the reality of who the couple is and let that story capture your wish for them. For instance, in the section in this book on "what is a wedding" I related the story of the older couple whose dancing moved me. I told that story at the ceremony of a couple that had met at a dance in high school. In my "words of good cheer," I shared the story, much as I've written it and spun my wish for the couple from it, i.e. that 40 years from now, may they still be each other's eyes, still dancing through life together. I went on to say my hope was that just like that dancing couple they'd always know the other was just an arm's length away through all life's journey.

After the ceremony, several people thanked me for the story. They said they could relate to it and most of these people went on to share with me some special memory that my story had evoked for them. That's the power of a good story – it stirs up other stories.

A solid story always packs an emotional wallop. You share a history with your couple, so find a humorous + poignant story or anecdote and let it capture the essence of your wish for them. However, keep in mind that you are not offering a toast – or a roast! You are encouraging them and not embarrassing them.

And here's what is both the unique and odd thing about a wedding ceremony: Although you're speaking to the couple, it's not just to them that you're speaking. You're standing before a group of people, family and friends, who also want and need your words of good cheer.

If you're not comfortable telling a story, then find a quote, a poem or a song lyric – something that speaks to the essence of your couple. Let that inspire your words – which should be brief!

Your words of good cheer should be no more than three to four minutes TOPS. During those minutes, connect with people's hearts.

REMEMBER: this is a prime spot where you can make the ceremony personal and romantic.

Exchange Of Vows

This is the heart of the ceremony. It is why everyone dropped what they were doing and came to the celebration.

When creating a ceremony one of the main issues I discuss with a couple is the vows. Ironically, most couples are most nervous about this element. Couples often tell me that they don't like standing in front of people who are looking at them. Well, that's going to be a hard one to get around at a wedding with any guests!

Couples Have 4 Options For Saying Their Vows
(Bonus Section has a selection of traditional vows)

Option #1: The couple selects a version of the traditional vows and then you phrase the vow as a question, asking each, individually, "Do you take _____to be your wife/husband. . ." and they each respond "I Do!" The problem, though, is that if someone sneezes, the vow is gone!

Option #2: The couple repeats after you the vows they've selected – hopefully you'll go as slow as they need you to!

Option #3: The couple writes their own vows. Many couples, though, are afraid to write their vows for fear they'll sound cheesy. I can honestly say that I've never heard vows that I thought were "cheesy." Granted, some were more eloquently worded than others, yet all were poignant.

I remind couples of how great it is that they have someone in their life that compels them to search deep in their heart for words that express the passion of their commitment.

I tell couples that they can be nervous about hundreds of eyes staring at them – but they don't have to be nervous about saying something lame. The committed heart is not able to offer cheesy sentiments!

Option #4: Some people get nervous at the thought of writing their own vows, even though they wish they could. They panic – what do I say? How do I write them? This 4th Option is a combination of both the personal and the traditional.

Sometimes people want to take a moment to say something personal to their partner, though it's not necessarily couched as a "vow" vow. These are simply words of gratitude, appreciation and love. Then, immediately after saying personal words to each other, they repeat a traditional vow after you.

Their words must be written down. No one expects a couple to have anything memorized, not even their names! I suggest they get a journal book. One person can write their sentiments in the front and the other in the back. At the appropriate time, you first give the book to the groom and he reads his thoughts to the bride; then, she takes the book and reads hers to the groom. When she's done, you take the book and continue on by having them repeat after you a traditional vow.

If the couple chooses to write their words on separate sheets of paper, the groom can keep his in his pocket and you can get the bride's beforehand so as to give it to her in the ceremony.

If, before the ceremony, the couple tells you that they're not up to saying their own words, then you have them repeat traditional vows and no one knows that they backed out of their original plan.

How long should the vows or personal words be? I am asked this question all the time – and I have no definitive answer! The vows / personal words are not a pre-nup – there is no way a couple can fully express what is in their hearts. Their words are but an echo of what is in their hearts. Some couples set a word limit or decide how many sentences each will say. This structure gives them freedom to be creative.

No matter what a couple decides, they should not show their vows to each other ahead of time. Their vows are a gift!

How To Introduce The Exchange Of Vows

In a church setting there are various formulations for introducing the exchange of vows called the "declaration of intent." However, I find these clichéd for a personalized ceremony. I use the following set piece (others are found in the Bonus Section):

"Marriage begins in the giving of words. We cannot give ourselves over to the other without giving our word. This must be an unconditional giving for in giving ourselves over to the other, we give ourselves over to the mystery that is love & life. And so it is, we, your family and friends, with open hearts, now bear witness, as you give your word, which is your life to each other."

NOTE: Guests are disappointed if they can't hear the vows; after all, that's why they've come to the ceremony. If the groom is wearing a lapel mic, he'll be heard when he says his vows; however, the bride will have to lean in at an awkward angle in order for her to be heard. So, I prefer using a hand-held mic that allows me to hold the mic close to the bride and groom when they say their vows. If they're repeating after me, I say the vow in a low voice, so people don't hear me; otherwise it begins to sound like a ventriloquist!

What To Say After The Couple Has Exchanged Their Vows

In a ceremony that is celebrated in the presence of God you can say:
"You have declared your consent before the community of your family and friends. May God ever gracious strengthen your consent and fill you both with abundant blessings. Pause. Whom God has joined, let no one divide."

In a non-religious ceremony, I'll say:
"You have spoken from hearts and pledged your word and your life to each other and I say,'So be it!'"

Vow Of The People

One way to involve family and friends is to invite them to make a "vow" to the couple. After the couple say their vows, I then ask all present:
"Do you promise to continue to love, nurture and support Jill and Jack in their life together? If so, shout out, WE WILL!"
And the guests roar, "We will!"

Guests appreciate the opportunity to voice their love within the context of the ceremony.
Note: this really only works with a lively, high-energy group!

Vow To Children

If the couple has children, one way to incorporate them into the ceremony is by having the couple make a "vow" to the children. I ask the couple, *"Do you promise to continue to love, nurture and support (names of children) and help them to become all that they are meant to be? If so, say WE DO!"* Sometimes the couple will also give the children a small gift, i.e. some kind of jewelry.

Exchange Of Rings

Before the couple exchanges their rings, the rings have to be presented to you. I officiated a wedding where the bride's cousin presented the rings while doing a belly dance with a sword balanced atop her head! Here, though, are some less exotic options.

Although many ceremonies have an adorable ring bearer, who hasn't a clue as to what's going on, the rule of thumb is if the ring bearer isn't old enough to legally drink a beer, then he/she isn't old enough to carry the real rings. However, if the couple wants to entrust their rings to a four-year old, then – so be it!

There are various ways in which to get the rings to you that personalize the ceremony and add emotional depth.

The most traditional custom is for the Best Man to have both rings. Contemporary traditional is for the Best Man and the Maid Of Honor to each have a ring.

Other variations include the last attendant on either side (groomsman, bridesmaid) each having a ring and at the appropriate time, when you ask for the rings, they pass them down to each member of the wedding party. The visual symbol here is that each person is affirming and confirming the couple in their life together.

If there is no wedding party, then the rings should be presented by someone(s) who has a meaningful connection to the couple. For instance, I've had both sets of parents present the rings OR both mothers OR both fathers. In one case, the bride was abandoned by both her parents and was raised by her grandmother and so it was the grandmother who presented the rings.

If the couple has children who are older than toddlers, and who are not in the wedding party, they could present the rings as a sign of their love for their parents (no need for you to verbally explain this meaning, as it is visually understandable).

However presented, the rings are handed to you. You invite the couple to join hands and then you say something of the significance of the rings (check Bonus #8). You then hand to the groom the ring he is about to give to his bride. As you hand him the ring, whisper the words he will say as he places the ring on the bride's finger (check Bonus #9). You then hand the bride the ring she's gifting to the groom and again whisper the words.

Oftentimes the couple is in such a daze that they don't even remember which hand or finger to place the ring. And sometimes the ring does not easily go on. All of this is an opportunity for you to make a light-hearted comment and break the nervousness!

Ring Warming Ceremony

This is a more elaborate way of presenting the rings and involves all the guests. At the beginning of the ceremony, after Words Of Welcome, I remind family and friends that the couple stands before them grateful for all of their love and support. Indeed, it is that love and support that has helped the couple come to this moment in time.

I remind everyone that the couple has invited them to bear witness to their vows and, in so doing, seeks their ongoing pledge of support and love.

I tell all present that the couple invites them to "warm" the rings they will give to each other as a pledge of their love. The rings, now in a pouch, will be passed along during the ceremony and each person is invited to hold the pouch briefly and offer a silent wish, hope or prayer.

I then hand the pouch containing the rings to the Best Man, who now begins this "warming of the rings." He passes it on to the groomsman next to him and on down the row of groomsmen.

The last groomsman brings the ring pouch to the groom's mother who then passes it on to the father (or whoever is sitting next to her).

The groomsman is the "guardian of the rings," as he will guide their passage as they weave their way through the guests.

When the last person in the last row "warms" the rings, the groomsman brings it to the other side and so it goes until the pouch reaches the bridesmaids.

By the time I reach the Exchange of Rings moment, the pouch, hopefully, will have reached the Maid Of Honor, who then hands me the rings. So far, I've been lucky!

Note: This works well with smaller weddings (50 people range). Once the pouch is handed to the Best Man, I continue on with the ceremony, as it would be a buzz-kill if the ceremony stopped while people just watched the bag being passed.

Once the rings have made their way back to you, you want to say something about their significance. Again, keep it short and poetic and don't turn it into a metaphysical lecture on the symbolism of the never-ending circle! (Bonus Section #8)

Hand Washing Ritual

Several years ago I officiated the wedding of Rob & Amber, Survivor show sweethearts who got married on the beach in the Bahamas. Their ceremony was unique not just because it was aired on television. After they exchanged vows (and prior to exchanging rings) I invited their mothers to come forward and wash Rob & Amber's hands. The water was in a shell-covered bowl; the Best Man and the Maid Of Honor assisted the mothers. It was a loving, symbolic act on the part of the mothers.

After the mothers washed and dried the hands of their respective child, they returned to their seats and Rob & Amber proceeded with the Exchange Of Rings.

Unity Rituals

After the Exchange Of Vows and The Exchange Of Rings, the couple has done what they came to do! Everything is now "icing on the cake." Sometimes couples like to perform a unity ritual and/or a ritual that honors their families – rituals that add symbolic richness and texture to the ceremony.

These rituals provide opportunity for the couple to personalize their ceremony and to incorporate any cultural or religious traditions. The rituals speak to the symbolic reality of the unity of the couple, or the uniting and honoring of their families.

I don't think a ceremony should be "cluttered" with too many of these rituals as they all speak to the same symbolic reality, i.e. the union and strength of the couple and their rootedness in family.

Since these are symbolic actions, they should make sense without needing prolonged explanations. A symbol only works as a symbol if no lengthy explanation is needed. Besides, definitions are not romantic!

I use these rituals and traditions as an opportunity to encourage the couple and to reassure them of our ongoing love and support.

NOTE: I'm listing these rituals here, after the Exchange Of Rings; however, some couples prefer a unity ritual / family ritual prior to their Exchange Of Vows, so that the ceremony can quickly conclude after the Exchange Of Rings. Again, it's simply a matter of what the couple prefers.

Here is a sampling of some time-honored and cherished rituals. Your couple may have different rituals they want to incorporate; however this section will give you ideas on how to weave ritual into the overall ceremony.

The Unity Candle

I spoke of the Unity Candle in my section on "What Is A Wedding." Again, what I do is I introduce this segment with a quote from a mystic that begins, "from every human being there rises a light" and I remind all present that it is such a love we celebrate today. I then turn to the couple and say, *"May the light and peace that shines on you today, always shine brightly on your life together."* They then light the candle. During this time, soft music can be playing.

NOTE: I avoid any explanation such as, "And now, as a symbol of their united, shining life together, Jack & Jill will light their candle. . ." Why verbally explain what is visually understandable?

Logistics: The Unity Candle consists of three candles – two taper candles and one tall, chunky candle placed between the tapers. The candles should be placed on a small, bistro-sized table either behind or off to the side of where you and the couple are standing. Remember matches or lighters!

If the ceremony is outdoors, then it is VERY IMPORTANT that the three candles be shielded with what's called "hurricane lamps." These are glass coverings that go around the candles and shelter them from breeze. You find these at stores such as Pottery Barn.

Also, the candles' wicks MUST be deep inside the hurricane lamps so that they don't blow out during the ceremony.

Just before the start of the ceremony, the tapers are lit, so they're burning throughout. They can be lit in one of two ways. Either you or the coordinator can light them prior to ceremony start OR, the mothers can light them at the beginning of the ceremony. During the time of PROCESSION, when both mothers have been escorted to their seats, they then come forward and light the candles. When they return to their seats, the Processional continues. Again, the symbolism here is of the families "blessing" the couple, though no verbal explanation is needed.

Variation On The Unity Candle

This variation only works indoors (check if venue permits lit candles as many don't). Each guest is given a candle taper when they arrive. At the time of the Unity Candle Ritual, I remind everyone that their love shines brightly on the couple and their being present at the ceremony is a valued pledge of their ongoing support.

Then, the candles of the last person sitting in the last rows on either side of the aisle are lit (logistics are to be worked out by you and the coordinator). These guests light the candle of the person next to them and the flame is passed from guest to guest on up through the wedding party until the lights reach the bride and groom.

The couple then lights their Unity Candle with what essentially is the collective light of family and friends. Music can play throughout this ritual.

Sand Ritual

Traditionally, in this popular ritual, the couple each has a vase of different colored sand (that perfectly match the color scheme of the wedding!) and together they pour their sand into a larger bowl, symbolizing their union.

I've expanded on this ritual, giving it a twist that incorporates family and friends. It goes like this:

When guests arrive, at the sign-in table are two glass bowls/vases – one empty and one with clear, beach-colored sand. Each guest is invited to place a small scoop of sand into the empty bowl. A card on the table reads:
"As a symbol of your care & love, we invite you to place a scoop of sand into this vase, which will become an honored part of our ceremony. Thank you!"

Then, before the start of the ceremony, the "guest" bowl is brought up to a table near where the couple and I will be standing. On that table will be two narrow vases, each containing different colored sand.

At the appropriate time, I hold up the "guest" bowl and remind everyone that in ways known and unknown to them, it is their love that has helped to bring the couple to this moment in time. The couple's life together is built on the love of all present. I mention that this bowl will have an honored place in their home, reminding them of all our hopes and love. The couple then pours their sand into the "guest" bowl.

In some ceremonies, the couple then go on to present their mothers with roses, so that this plays out as a seamless unit. It begins with the larger acknowledgement of friends and family and ends with the intimate show of respect and gratitude to the parents.

Rose Ceremony Honoring Mothers

If each person is close to their own parents and in particular to their respective mothers, then one way they can honor their families is by giving each of the mothers a long-stemmed rose or some appropriate flower. The fathers don't expect anything, as mother is the symbol of family. However, one couple gave each of the fathers a bottle of Tequila!

I introduce this segment by recognizing that the couple is grateful to all present for their friendship and support. Indeed, it is their love that has helped to bring them to this moment in time. I go on to say that the couple is especially grateful for the unwavering support, encouragement and sacrifice of their parents. Then, they go together first to the bride's mother and the bride gives her mother a rose – kiss-kiss, hug-hug, sniffle–sniffle and then, together, they go to the groom's mother and he gives her a rose – kiss-kiss, hug-hug, sniffle–sniffle! They then return to me.

Wine Box Ritual

I suggest this ritual to a couple who isn't into sand, but who enjoys a good glass of wine! Before their wedding, the couple gets a bottle of their favorite wine, a wine box (or any ornamental box big enough to hold a bottle of wine, think Pottery Barn, etc.) and they write a letter to each other – a letter of love and gratitude.

Before the ceremony, the wine, the box and the letters are placed on a small bistro table near us.

I introduce this segment by explaining that the couple have written these letters and will tuck them into the box along with the wine. They're not going to open the wine or read the letters until either their first or fifth wedding anniversary (couple decides).

I remind the couple that tucked into the box is also all of our love and hopes and wishes. I also urge people to look for the box when they visit the couple at home and make sure they've not opened the bottle!

The couple then places the wine and letters into the box and closes it. Some couples actually seal the box with nails; most find this a bit too funereal!

You can further incorporate family and friends, by having the wine box at the sign-in table along with small note cards and pens. Each guest is invited to write a wish and place it in the box. Then, just before the ceremony start, the box is brought up to that bistro table near where you and the couple will be standing.

Other variations include the couple asking just their parents to write them a letter and then having them place those letters in the box. I've also had couples ask each person in their wedding party to write them a letter. At the rehearsal the bride's attendants' letters are tied together, as are the groom's attendants' letters and then in the ceremony, the Best Man and Maid Of Honor place those packets in the box.

Another couple got three bottles of wine and a box made to accommodate the bottles. The couple placed in the box their bottle (to be opened on their 1st anniversary), then the bride's parents presented a bottle (for their 5th anniversary), followed by the groom's parents who presented a bottle (for their 10th anniversary).

The point is – be creative and have fun!

In some ceremonies, after closing the box, the couple go on to present their mothers with roses, so that this plays out as a seamless unit.

Signing Of The Marriage License By Witnesses

Typically, the witnesses (usually the Best Man and Maid Of Honor) and officiant sign the marriage license after the ceremony. However, sometimes couples want the license signed during the ceremony, in the presence of family and friends, so that all give witness to this act.

I introduce this segment by explaining that while I'm the official legal witness along with the Maid Of Honor and Best Man (if they're the people the couple want to sign as witnesses), the reality is that the three of us affix out signatures in the name of all present.

I then remind everyone that the couple invited each one of them to the ceremony because they wanted them to witness the giving of their vows. In that spirit of witnessing, the license is signed in the presence of all.

Usually, a small table is off to the side and either the table is brought to the center or the three of us go to the table.

Religious / Cultural Traditions

Various cultures have distinct wedding ceremony traditions varying by religion and/or ethnicity.

Catholic

Cultures influenced by the Spanish Catholic Church have symbolic rituals involving: Thirteen Gold Coins (Arras), The Cord and The Veil.

Thirteen Gold Coins – Arras

The groom gifts his bride with thirteen gold coins (Arras) that represent Christ and the 12 Apostles. Traditionally, in gifting his bride with The Arras, the groom pledges to be a good provider and to support and care for her as his wife. By accepting the coins, the bride offers the groom her mutual trust and support.

Usually, I do the Coin Ritual before the Exchange of Vows and Exchange of Rings. I call the Coin Sponsor (godparent) up by name. I then explain that before the couple exchanges their vows, according to revered tradition, the godparent presents to the groom these 12 Arras. I then say to the couple, *"May the giving and receiving of these coins remind and reassure you of your pledge to mutually care for each other in a daily spirit of trust and confidence."*

The Sponsor hands me the thirteen coins (in a pouch or box), which I drop into the groom's hands. In turn, he drops them into the bride's hands. She returns them to the groom, who places them back on the tray or into the box/pouch that is held by the Sponsor. The Sponsor places them on a table set-up near us.

Once the ritual is completed, I proceed with The Exchange Of Vows as I've outlined.

Lazo – Lasso

A lazo (lasso) is a large rosary or a white, knotted cord that is draped around the necks and shoulders of the bride and the groom. It's placed in a horizontal figure eight (infinity) to affirm their commitment to be together side-by-side throughout life.

I incorporate the Lazo at the end of the ceremony, in preparation for the Final Blessing. I call the Cord Sponsors (different from the Coin Sponsor) up by name. They drape the couple with the "cord" and take a step back. I then read these verses from the Book of Ecclesiastes:

"If one falls, the other can help the companion up again; but alas for the one who falls alone with no partner to help. And if two lie side by side, they keep each other warm; but how can a person keep warm by oneself? If a person is alone, an enemy may overpower them, but two can resist. And a rope of three strands is not quickly snapped."

I remind the couple that it is our prayer that the bonds of their love will not easily be broken and that God will be generous in giving them strength in the good times and the bad.

I give them a Final Blessing after which the Sponsors remove the cord and return to their seats. I then "pronounce and present" the couple as husband and wife.

The Veil

Another tradition is The Veil. If the couple chooses to include The Veil, then I call up The Veil Sponsors (again, a different set) who place the veil around the groom's shoulder and over the bride's head. The veil is a reminder that now 'clothed' as one, the couple is to be a shelter and protection for each other.

In a church wedding, the Veil Sponsors first drape the veil and then the Cord Sponsors drape the cord over the couple. However, for the sake of simplicity, I suggest that the couple select just either the cord or the veil.

The Sponsors step aside, I give a blessing, then the Sponsors remove the veil, return to their seats, and I "pronounce and present" the couple as husband and wife.

Jewish

The iconic symbols in the Jewish tradition are the Chuppah and the Breaking Of The Glass.

Chuppah

In a Jewish wedding ceremony the couple stand under a Chuppah (canopy). The Chuppah is traditionally made from a tallit (prayer shawl) or a decorated square of cloth held up by four poles. The poles are either supported in the ground or are held up by honored family and friends throughout the ceremony. The Chuppah, which symbolizes the couple's new home together, is open on all sides, so as to welcome friends and family.

I've seen floral designers create exquisite natural Chuppahs and I've stood under Chuppahs that were patch-works from treasured heirlooms from both families. This is an opportunity for the couple to further personalize. While deeply rooted in Jewish tradition, the Chuppah now has a decorative and practical purpose as it serves as shelter from the sun for an outdoor wedding!

In a religious Jewish ceremony, the couple and their rabbi stand inside the Chuppah. For the purposes of a non-religious ceremony, I have the couple stand in front of the Chuppah, so all can see them.

Breaking of the Glass

This is an ancient and revered Jewish nuptial tradition. It comes at the very end of the ceremony, after you've pronounced the couple husband and wife. While it has many meanings and interpretations, this is how I incorporate it:

At the end of the ceremony, just prior to the Final Blessing, I invite everyone to stand. I explain that in a moment, I will pronounce the couple husband and wife, and then, after their Kiss, the groom, according to ancient Jewish wedding tradition, will break the glass.
I tell the couple that I want them to know that our deepest wish is that it:
"May be harder to break the bond of your love, harder than it would be to put back these shards of broken glass."

I then place the glass, wrapped in a cloth or pouch, on the ground between the groom and bride, remind him not to do anything just yet, and proceed with my words of blessing. I then Pronounce and Present them as husband and wife. They kiss. Break the glass. All shout, "Mazel Tov!"

Asian

Tea Ceremony Honoring Family

Based on culture and nationality, there are many variations to the traditional Tea Ceremony. In its pure form, the ceremony is highly ritualistic and takes place the morning of the wedding.

Couples who incorporate the ceremony into their public wedding do so in a streamlined, modified form.

Near where the couple is standing will be a small table. On the table there will be:
tea tray, tea pot and cups for each of the honored family members.

During the ceremony, the Maid Of Honor stays at the table and pours the tea. The Best Man carries the tray and accompanies the couple as they go first to the groom's family. The parents and honored relatives remain seated. The couple bow. The bride presents tea to the groom's father, mother and any honored relatives. When done, the Best Man returns to the table, deposits the used cups and with the help of the maid of honor places the new teacups on the tray and returns to the couple. The couple now has crossed over to the bride's family and the ritual is repeated. Once completed, the Best Man returns the tea tray to the small table while the couple takes their place again in front of me.

African-American

Jumping The Broom

Jumping the broom is a custom with deep meaning going back to the days of U.S. slavery when slaves weren't allowed to legally marry. As a public declaration of their love and commitment, a slave couple would jump over a decorated broom, symbolically entering the Holy Land of Marriage, sweeping away evil from their life together.

Today, some couples see this as a symbolic ritual in which they leave behind their past life of aloneness and together jump into their shared future. Usually, I will explain the ritual's history and assure the couple that as they leap into the future, all of our love and hopes go with them. I place the broom on the ground; I offer a Final Blessing or Sending Forth and then I Pronounce and Present them as a husband and wife. They kiss and immediately Jump The Broom.

I once officiated a wedding for a couple where the bride was Jewish and the groom was African-American Christian. They incorporated BOTH the Breaking Of The Glass and Jumping The Broom. I explained each tradition and then set the broom on the ground with the glass just beyond it. I zapped them with a blessing; pronounced and presented them as husband and wife. They kissed, Jumped The Broom AND then smashed the glass. All shouted "Mazel Tov."

There are many other cultural traditions, religious and non-religious, that can be woven into a ceremony so as to make it highly personal to the couple.

Remember: The "trick" is to honor the culture and/or religion by seamlessly weaving a signature moment in such a way that it doesn't appear out-of-place, so that it doesn't disrupt the flow of the ceremony or bring about a sense of "dueling deities." The ritual should be the visual manifestation of a collective hope for the couple. Don't make the rituals so complicated that they're awkward and messy looking. The couple will be in an altered state of mind and YOU are going to have to guide them through it all!

Favorite Cross-Cultural, Interfaith Wedding

The bride was Mexican Catholic and the groom was Jewish from Philadelphia. The bride's mother was ill and so they decided to have the wedding in her family's hometown, an hour outside Mexico City. The wedding was held at a resort whose main building was 450 years old and had been built by Cortez as a gift to his mistress.

The ceremony took place in a private courtyard near a 200-year old mission chapel. A Chuppah was set up (no one on staff at the resort had ever seen a Chuppah) and underneath the Chuppah was a table that served as the "altar" of sorts. It had, though, a hidden, practical purpose. The groom was prone to anxiety attacks, especially when having to be the center of attention in front of a large group. The table was a physical reassurance for him and that let him mentally center himself physically.

In the far corner, still under the Chuppah, was a statue of Our Lady of Guadalupe, patron of Mexican Catholics.

The couple had readings in Spanish and English. They presented roses to their mothers and while they did so, the bride's uncle, a noted Mexican actor, sang Ave Maria. Prior to the final blessing, the bride's godparents draped them with the veil and cord, and I offered an ancient Jewish blessing. When I pronounced them husband and wife, the groom stomped the glass, all shouted Mazel Tov, and the Mariachi Band kicked in!

These were simple rituals that did not compete with each other. No dueling deities. Family and friends resolved to focus on what united them rather than what divided them.

2nd Reading

Sometimes the couple cannot choose between two readings and opt to include both in the ceremony. In that case, the second reading, which should be the shorter of the two, can come right before the Sending Forth / Blessing. Think of it as a bow on a package!

Sending Forth / Blessing

It is now time to bring the ceremony to its conclusion. You ask all present to stand and then do one of two options:

Option #1: You send the couple forth into the world with everyone's love to live out their lives, without mentioning God, and so this is technically not a "blessing." These final words of encouragement urge the couple to live out their lives, fulfilling the promise of this great day.

Option #2: You send the couple forth into the world with everyone's love to live out their lives AND with God's blessing.

It all depends on the religious and spiritual sensibilities of the couple.

No matter which option is used, I introduce either the blessing or the "sending forth" with a word of gratitude to the couple. In the name of all, I thank them for the gift of this day – a day that reminds us that life is good and worthy of our best. It's in that spirit of gratitude that I then bless / send them forth. (See Bonus Sections #11 and #12)

Pronouncement Of Marriage

Traditionally, after the Blessing or Sending Forth, the officiant pronounces the couple married with the words, "By the power vested in me by the State of _____, I now pronounce you husband and wife."

This is followed by the first kiss of the newly married couple, when the officiant says, "You may now kiss."

Presentation Of The Newlyweds

After the kiss, the officiant then introduces the couple, saying, "I present to you Mr. and Mrs. _____" or "I present to you the newly married couple, Jack and Jill."

What I've described above is the most traditional way to conclude the ceremony. However, I typically do it a different way.

Immediately after the Sending Forth or Blessing, I pronounce the couple husband and wife and introduce them at the same time. My own wording is:

"By the power vested in me, it is my honor to pronounce as, and to present for the first time, as husband and wife. . ."
Here you have options (from most formal to least formal):
Mr. & Mrs. Smith
Mr. & Mrs. John Smith
Mr. & Mrs. John and Jill Smith
John and Jill Smith

OR, some couples want to do away with using the last name and prefer, John and Jill – husband and wife.

Kiss

Immediately after pronouncing and presenting them, I then say: "Now you may kiss!"

I IMMEDIATELY step aside as soon as I say, "Now you may kiss" so that the photo shot is just of the couple – photographers will thank you.

Release Of Doves / Butterflies

For dramatically romantic effect, some couples have doves or butterflies released as they are kissing. It makes for a great photo; however, it's your responsibility to make sure that the photographer, musicians, and person in charge of releasing the winged creatures know their cue.
Also, there are various explanations for the symbolism behind the doves or butterflies. My own preference is to let the visual speak for itself. There is, though, a charming legend about the release of butterflies that does need explaining:

"Indian legend says that if you whisper a wish to a captured butterfly and then release it, your wish will come true. The belief is that the released butterfly will share your wish with the Great Spirit."

When the couple chooses to incorporate this legend, I invite an honored relative or friend, who the couple has asked to be "Guardian Of The Butterflies," to come up before the Final Blessing /Sending Forth. I explain the legend and then ask all to take a moment and make a silent wish/prayer for the couple. I then offer my blessing / sending forth, and immediately after my words the butterflies are released. I pronounce and present the couple as husband and wife. They kiss.

Recessional

Strike up the music! The bride retrieves her bouquet from the Maid Of Honor and the couple recesses back up the aisle, followed by the wedding party, the bride's parents, the groom's parents and then you.

Post Ceremony

Prior to ceremony start, check with Coordinator if they'd like you to make an announcement regarding who should stay behind for photos or if they'd like you to point guests in direction of the Reception.

Right after the ceremony, I nab the best man and maid of honor (or whoever the couple has chosen as their witnesses) and have them sign the license. It is your responsibility to sign and mail back the license to the County Clerk's office.

PART 3

HOW TO DELIVER THE CEREMONY

Conducting a wedding ceremony is a unique form of public speaking. As ritual, a wedding ceremony has several aspects that make it distinct from any other kind of presentation.

You're standing in front of what are often two nervous wrecks, so you have to be their rock and emotional support throughout the ceremony. As their rock, you need to keep in mind that:

1. Although this is one of the most intimate moments in the couple's life, it's being played out in front of a group of people in a public setting.
2. Although the ceremony is very much about the couple, your words are not just for them alone – you have a larger audience and the ceremony is really a gift to family and friends.
3. Although you are the official legal witness (hence, officiant), the guests are also present as witnesses, and you need to remind them of that role and honor throughout the ceremony.
4. Although your "title" is officiant, what you really are is the "host" of the ceremony. Your job is to guide the couple and their guests through the various moments of this emotionally-charged experience.

Recognizing all this, the single most important thing for you to keep in mind is that while you can have a well-structured ceremony and you can have heart-felt, inspiring words, if you don't deliver them with equal feeling, enthusiasm, conviction and passion, then it all falls flat.

Remember: in every situation, all of what we communicate simultaneously takes place on two levels. Content and Tone.

We often think that if our content (words) is solid, then the way in which we present it (tone) doesn't matter. However, a full 80% of what we pay attention to in any encounter is the non-verbal, i.e. tone of voice, pacing, facial and body expressions. Only 20% of what we pay attention to is actually the "what" of what is being said!

What does this mean for you? It means you have to:

Be Prepared. Be You. Be Engaging.

Be Prepared

There's so much you want to say to the couple because they mean the world to you. However, more is not better! You can't say everything that's in your heart, so choose your words with care.

Avoid the clichés. It's ALL about the emotions! Make an emotional connection with the couple, their family and friends. Story, anecdote, image, lively words, participation and movement all go towards creating an "experience."

If you've never conducted a ceremony, or if you're not used to speaking in public, then you must write out your script. You can't ad-lib a wedding ceremony!

Plan how you're going to introduce each moment. Make sure you know how you're going to transition from segment to segment.

Transitions give smooth flow to the ceremony. You need to transition from one moment in the ceremony to the next. Sometimes a smile and a dramatic Pause will do it. Other times, you need a sentence or two to move all into the next moment.

Unless you know how to read your own handwriting, print out the ceremony in easy-to-read format. Double-space. Mark it up and make it your clear road-map for everything that is going to take place in the ceremony.

Have your ceremony script in a nice looking book or binder that is easy for you to hold and whose pages turn easily. Avoid anything that's too bulky or too school-ish looking. Make sure the color of the book's cover compliments the bride's color scheme – trust me, she'll thank you! You could even put your script on an i-Pad or tablet.

Knowing your audience is part of your preparation. You may know the groom's or bride's family better than the other family and so it's important to consider ALL the relatives in the audience. You may have spent college years carousing with the groom or bride, but this is not the time to regale folks with embarrassing stories. The time for that is at the rehearsal dinner or during reception toasts. Don't give grandma a heart attack!

In the days leading up to the ceremony, continue to prepare, fine-tune and review your material. Be VERY familiar with the structure and flow of the ceremony; make sure you know the names of the people who have a role in the ceremony and be comfortable with the cues you'll be giving them. Memorize your opening and closing words. This especially makes a difference.

Be You

The couple has invited you to officiate because you hold a special place in their hearts and they believe you can add something that a hired officiant can't. Too often, people think that the wedding must be "solemn," because it is a serious undertaking. People then act in a forced way. Be you. Be real, authentic and communicate through your feelings.

The ONLY way you can be comfortable enough to be "you" in the ceremony is if you're prepared! I can't emphasize enough the importance of preparation. Starting the week before the wedding is too late. You have just one opportunity to give them the ceremony of a lifetime.

Be Engaging

In general, presentations are dreadful because we are so focused on content that we forget about what people really respond to, i.e. the non-verbal. Paying attention to the details of how you present and host the ceremony will go a long way in helping you connect with people.

Non-Verbal Essentials

Eye Contact: When you make eye contact with people as you speak, you build a bond with them. You emotionally connect through eye contact. Memorize your opening words and deliver them looking at the couple and their guests as this will make everyone feel you're talking to them and not at them.

Smile: No one is judging you. It's a wedding and not a funeral.

Body Orientation: When the couple stands in front of you, make sure they're facing each other so the guests can see their profile. If the microphone is on a stand, adjust it to the correct height so you're not leaning down and into it. With solid preparation, you won't have to be glued to your book and you can stand straight and look directly at the couple and their guests.

Space: Oftentimes couples don't know how to stand or what to do in the ceremony. Amazing, but true! Make sure they're not standing far apart from each other. I usually suggest they hold hands. The three of you want to stand close enough to the front row of seats so that an intimacy is created, though you don't want to be so close that you're in their laps. And if you are standing in front of an arch, make sure the flowers don't droop on you. I've had photos taken of me where it looks like I've got roses sprouting out of my head!

Voice & Pacing: Be animated – avoid speaking in monotone. Don't rush! Pause between thoughts so as to emphasize what you're saying. You're taking this group of people on a journey, so have fun with it all. There's no hurry. Pause for dramatic effect. Pause so guests can think about what you've just said.

Dress: Ask the bride for her preference in terms of what you wear, i.e. suit and tie? Dress? Length? Color? I typically wear a black suit, white shirt and my tie compliments the groom and his groomsmen. You don't want your clothes to distract from the bride and groom.

How To Manage Your Nerves

Although I've officiated hundreds of weddings, I still get nervous before each ceremony. And that's okay. I should feel nervous, as each ceremony is a big deal! No two weddings are alike because no two couples are alike. Each wedding has its own feel and "vibe." Part of my job is to be aware of and in tune with the overall tone of the gathering. Over time, I've found ways to manage my nerves and let them work to my benefit. You've probably heard these tips before, as they are tried and true:

Breathe: Doubts cause nerves that, in turn, cause shallow breathing, or even holding of your breath. Remember to breathe and remember that this is all about the couple – not you.

Bluff: Stand tall, shoulders back, feet planted firmly on the ground. Smile. Your body physically tricks your brain into feeling confident. I'm not a scientist, so I don't understand how this works, but it really does!

Keep you mouth and throat hydrated. A breath mint can do double duty.

Arrive Early: I always arrive an hour ahead of time. This way, I'm not rushing when I show up. I can relax, ease into the atmosphere. Handle any last minute details. Touch base with the people who are part of the ceremony.

AND I can go off to a spot and collect my thoughts and review the ceremony one last time – which is for me the most important part of final prep. Sorry, but you don't have time to hang out with the groom or bride or their families (even if you are family) BECAUSE you have a job to do. Focus on your job!

BONUS #1

Wedding Ceremony In A Glance

A wedding ceremony is:

- A celebration of a couple's journey together – past, present future
- A time for all to recall what life is about – love, loyalty, family, friends
- An act of gratitude
- An emotional experience
- A touchstone for a couple's life and the creating of a "collective memory"

When done well, a ceremony:

- Sets the tone for the reception party
- Propels people into the party
- Reminds people what it is they're celebrating

3 Elements Of A Ceremony

Structure:

- Organize flow of ceremony
- Keep it simple
- Keep it under 30 minutes from start to kiss
- Keep focus on Vows + Rings as heart of the ceremony
- Select what you want to have happen prior to the vows + rings
- Select what you want to have happen after the vows + rings
- Avoid ritual clutter

Content:

- Decide what you will say in each segment of the ceremony, i.e. introduction, words of good cheer, final words, words of pronouncement, etc.
- Decide the words you'll use to introduce each segment
- Decide the words you'll use to transition from one moment to another
- Write out your script, then edit, then familiarize
- Memorize opening and closing words

Delivery:

- Engage the gathering right from the beginning
- Avoid clichés, stuffy formulas, abstract concepts
- Personalize your words
- Don't preach
- Don't be a stand-up
- Don't drone on and on
- Pay attention to your non-verbal
- Have a mic so you can be heard
- Make sure the couple can be heard when they say their vows

Main Segments Of A Ceremony

Words Of Welcome:

- Introduce yourself
- Acknowledge reality of all present
- Invite your couple to soak it all in
- Invite guests to be in the moment
- Honor deceased
- Offer prayer if couple desires

Reading:

- Has two purposes: puts the brakes on ceremony and provides an opportunity to include special people
- Have no more than two readings
- Keep readings to under 90 seconds

Words Of Good Cheer:

- Remember you speak on behalf of all
- Be most personal
- Offer a story, an image that speaks to the reality of the couple and your wish for them and that packs an emotional wallop
- Do not give a PowerPoint presentation on "what is marriage"

Exchange Of Vows:

- Offer an introduction to this segment
- Invite couple to exchange vows
- Consider additional options of "Vow Of The People" and "Vow To Children"

Exchange Of Rings:

- Ask for the presentation of the rings
- Offer words that introduce this symbolic exchange
- Invite the couple to repeat after you as they exchanges rings

Texture: If couple prefers, some of these rituals can be done prior to the Exchange of Vows

- There are two main types of rituals – those that celebrate the couple's union and those that honor the couple's families
- Cultural and/or religious traditions can be seamlessly woven into the ceremony during this time
- Music can accompany rituals as they're being performed

Final Blessing or Sending Forth:

- Thank the couple for the gift of this day
- Bless them or send them forth in the name of all present – with gusto

Pronouncement And Presentation As Married:

- Make sure you do this with joy and flair

Kiss:

- As soon as you say, "Now you may kiss!" Step Aside!
- Immediately after the kiss is the time for smashing the glass, jumping the broom, release of the doves or butterflies

Recessional:

- As rehearsed by coordinator

Bonus #2

How To Avoid Turning The Ceremony Into A Lecture

People often think of the wedding ceremony as a ritual that must be done in a specific and solemn manner. This simply isn't true and it's important you understand this as you prepare to officiate your couple's wedding.

As I've written earlier, my belief is that a wedding is not the time to lecture the couple and their guests about the nature of marriage. Although well intentioned, professional and non-professional wedding celebrants drone on in lofty, abstract terms about love and commitment.

This is precisely what makes a wedding boring and your couple invited you to officiate their wedding because they don't want a boring ceremony.

The wedding ceremony is a ritual in which family and friends surround a couple with their love and support as the couple pledges to live out their life together in mutual love, courage and faithfulness. Period. It's that simple!

The ceremony is about wishing, encouraging, blessing and storytelling. And all of this should be done in a way that is uncomplicated, visually compelling and verbally engaging.

Remember: You, as the officiant, are the voice of everyone present. You are the voice of everyone's hopes, wishes, and blessings (if so understood). You also are the host of the ceremony and as such, you guide the couple and their guests through the ritual. That is what's asked of you.

Since you are the voice, avoid lengthy explanations of unity rituals that are riddled with clichés and trite expressions.

For instance, if you are introducing the Unity Candle, nix saying something like, "And now as a symbol of Jack and Jill pledging to live a united life together in the years ahead, they will light the Unity Candle which is a symbol of the purity of their commitment."

Rather, turn the Unity Candle into a moment for offering a hope and wish. Say something like, "Jack & Jill, as you light this Unity Candle, know that we all thank you for the gift of your love that shines brightly in all of our lives and know that it's our deepest hope that your love will continue to shine bright all the days of your life together." By turning the moment into a wish, everyone is now a part of the lighting.

The key is to trust that the symbol is visually powerful enough so that it doesn't need you to comment at length on the obvious. Let each ritual be an opportunity to offer a wish, a hope or a blessing. Ask yourself what is the wish you have for the couple based on the symbolism of the ritual being performed?

So, too, with rituals honoring family. Avoid saying, "And now, Jack & Jill will give their mothers a rose as a symbol of their love." Since people know that the rose is a symbol of love, simply say something like, "Jack and Jill stand before you grateful for all the love and sacrifice of their parents, for without them, there would be no today, etc." Then have the couple present the roses.

Whenever you say the phrase, "And now as a symbol of. . ." you're turning the ritual act into a lecture and that always kills the romance and poetry of the moment.

Some cultural and religious rituals can be incorporated into a larger moment. For instance, with The Veil or The Cord from the Spanish tradition, I always incorporate it as a part of the Final Blessing, rather than making it a moment on its own. Coupling it with the blessing enriches the symbolism.

A first time officiant I coached was confused when the couple told him that at the end of the ceremony, after he pronounced them married, they wanted to grab a pair of walking sticks and recess up the aisle. They're hikers and they thought it would make for a cute Instagram pic! Which it would, but to punch up the emotional impact of the moment, I suggested that the officiant hand them the sticks, remind guests of the couple's love of hiking and say something like, "Embrace the journey of you life together with courage and generosity and know that our love follows you wherever you go!" That was their "Sending Forth."

Bottom line: BE CREATIVE. Weave the symbols and rituals into the ceremony so that they don't stick-out in stand alone fashion. Don't cram too many rituals into the ceremony, as they will become redundant in meaning. Encourage the couple to select only those rituals and symbols that have strong personal meaning for them.

This is how you personalize a ceremony!

Bonus #3

Checklist: For Planning Ceremony With The Couple

1.   Is there anything the couple knows that they DO want; anything they know they DON'T want?

2.   Are there any deceased loved ones the couple wants to honor or have you mention in your Words of Welcome?

3.   Do they want to have a reading? Who will do the reading and how will it be read?

4.   How would they like to say their vows? Personal? Traditional? Personal + Traditional?

5.   Would they like their guests to do the "Vow of the People"?

6.   If the couple has children, how would they like them included? Vow to the Children?

7.   How would they like the rings to be presented? What would they like to say as they place the ring on each other's finger?

8.   Does the couple want any Unity / Honoring Family Ritual? Which ones? Who will be involved? Do they want music to accompany the ritual?

9.   Would the couple like a blessing or a non-religious "sending forth" at the end of the ceremony?

10.   Do they want to end the ceremony with any religious or cultural traditions such as smashing the glass or jumping the broom? Doves? Butterflies?

11.   What wording do they want for their introduction as a married couple?

12.   Who do they want to sign the license as their witnesses?

13.   What kind of outfit do they prefer you wear?

14.   Is there anything else the couple wants or they want you to be aware of?

Bonus #4

Checklist: Day of Ceremony

1. Arrive 1 hour early and check in with coordinator.

2. Touch base with the couple and make quick review of ceremony with them for any possible last minute changes.

3. If couple is doing their own vows, make sure they have their vows and keep bride's vows with you.

4. Get your hands on the marriage license and have witnesses sign if not before the ceremony, then immediately afterwards.

5. Who has the rings? Check with those responsible for presenting them.

6. Introduce yourself to the photographers and alert them to any special moments in the ceremony.

7. Introduce yourself to the videographer and alert them to any special moments in the ceremony.

8. Test the mic / adjust height if on a stand.

9. Speak to the readers. Make sure they have the readings (bring back-up copies). Remind them of their cues.

10. Check that all the elements for any Unity / Honoring Family Rituals are in place, i.e. roses, candles, sand, etc.

11. Check with the bride's escort and review if you're asking the "who presents?" question.

12. Give the musicians their cue for end of ceremony.

13. Review cues with the wranglers for doves or butterflies if needed.

14. NO BOOZE!

15. Don't hang out with wedding party or guests – focus!

16. Put your cell phone on "airplane mode."

17. Go off to a spot by yourself and make a quick review of the ceremony.

Bonus #5

Opening Prayers

#1

Lord, behold our family and friends here assembled.
We thank you for this place in which we celebrate:
For the love that it unites in us,
For the peace given to us this day,
For the hope with which we dream,
For the health, the work, the food,
And the bright skies that make our lives delightful,
For our friends and family, here present and away.
And most especially we thank you for N & N
Who today are united in marriage.
We ask now that you bless our celebration and
Bless our hearts that we may always
Bear witness to your generosity in our world. AMEN.

#2

Good and faithful God, we thank you for this great day.
We thank you for the gift of N &N, for the gift of their
Love in our lives.
Bless us all; bless our celebration and
Through what we do here today,
May we become ever clearer reflections of
Your compassion and graciousness in our world.
We ask this of you with hearts filled with faith, hope and love,
In the name of Jesus, your beloved, our lord and brother. AMEN.

Bonus #6

Intro To Vows

#1

But when two people are as one
In their innermost hearts,
They shatter even the strength
Of iron or bronze.
And when two people understand each other
In their innermost hearts,
Their words are sweet and strong
Like the fragrance of orchids.

~from the I Ching

#2

Marriage begins in the giving of your word. You cannot join yourselves to one another without giving your word. This must be unconditional giving, for in joining yourselves to each other, you join yourselves to tomorrow, the unknown and ever-changing season of life.

After reading one of the above selections, or words of your own, you then say something to the effect: *"And so it is, N & N, that we, your family and friends (in the presence of God), now bear witness as you give your word and pledge your love and your life to each other."* They then can repeat after you or say for themselves one of the following versions of the traditional vows (see section on Exchange Of Vows for other options the couple has for saying their vows).

Bonus #7

Traditional And Non-Traditional Vows

#1

I, __take you, __to be my wife/husband.
I promise to be true to you,
In good times and in bad,
In sickness and in health.
I will love you and honor you,
All the days of my life.
This is my solemn vow.

#2

I, __ take you, __to be my wife/husband
To have and to hold from this day forward,
For better for worse,
For richer, for poorer,
In sickness and in health,
To love and to cherish,
Until death do us part.

#3

I, __ take you, __ to be my wife/husband from this day forward.
In the presence of (God), our family and friends,
I offer you my solemn vow to be your faithful partner
In sickness and in health,
In good times and in bad,
In joy as well as sorrow.
I promise to love you unconditionally,
To support you in your goals,
To honor and respect you,
To laugh with you and cry with you, and
To cherish you for as long as we both shall live.

#4

I, __, take you, __, to be my wife/husband,
My partner in life and my one true love.
I will love you more each day than I did the day before.
I will trust and respect you,
Laugh with you and cry with you,
Loving you faithfully
Through good times and bad,
Regardless of the obstacles we may face.
I give you my hand, my heart, and my love
From this day forward
As long as we both shall live.

#5

I, __, take you, __, to be my wife/husband.
I embrace you with all your faults and strengths,
As I offer myself to you with all my faults and strengths.
I promise to cherish, respect, protect and comfort you.
I promise you my deepest love, my fullest devotion,
My most tender care.
You are my love and my life,
And with you I have found my home.

#6

I, __, take you, __, to be my wife/husband.
I will be yours in times of plenty and in times of want,
In times of sickness and of health,
In times of joy and of sorrow,
Failure and triumph.
I promise to cherish and respect you,
To protect and care for you,
Comfort and encourage you,
And to stay with you for all eternity.

#7

I, __, choose you, __, to be my wife/husband,
To respect you in your successes and in your failures,
To care for you in sickness and in health,
To nurture you and to grow with you
Throughout the seasons of our life together.
This is my joyful vow.

#8

I, __, take you, __, to be my partner,
Loving all that I know of you,
Trusting all that I do not yet know.
I embrace this gift to grow together,
To witness the woman/man you will become,
And to fall more in love with each passing day.
I promise to love, honor and cherish you
Throughout all that life will offer us,
All the days of our lives.

#9   in this version, the bride and groom alternate lines and together say the final line

Groom: Here we stand face-to-face and heart-to-heart
Bride: We make these vows as our own two lives unite
Groom: In the presence and love of our family and friends
Bride: A vow to listen and be understanding
Groom: A vow to be supportive and caring
Bride: A vow to respect and honor
Groom: A vow to cherish our times together
Bride: A vow to treasure our commitment to each other
BOTH: And a promise to love, honor and be together always and forever.

After the couple has said their vows, you can say either, "So be it!" an ancient expression of approval or, if the couple have taken their vows in the presence of God, you can say, *"I remind you that God abundantly blesses your love and whom God has joined let no one divide!"*

Bonus # 8

Intro To The "Exchange Of Rings"

In ancient times, it was believed that the vein on the fourth finger of the left hand led directly to the heart.

The rings will be presented to you in one of the ways described in the section on Exchange Of Rings. Once you have the rings you can read one of these passages as an Introduction.

#1

Everything the Power of the World does is done in a circle. The sky is round and the earth is round like a ball, and so are all the stars. The wind, in its greatest power, whirls. Birds make their nests in circles. The sun comes forth and goes down again in a circle. The moon does the same, and both are round. Even the seasons form a great circle in their changing, and always come back again to where they were. The life of a man and of a woman is a circle from childhood to childhood, and so it is in everything where power moves.
~Black Elk, Oglala Sioux

Intro: After reading this passage, hold out the rings to the couple and say something like: "May these rings remind you of the enduring power of your love and strengthen you throughout life's journey." Then you hand the groom the ring he's giving to his bride, and have him repeat after you, one of the versions of the Ring Exchange listed in the next section. With a same-sex couple, I suggest that the person who offered their vows second be the person to offer the ring first.

#2

Rings are an ancient symbol, blessed, simple, round,
Like the sun, like the eye, like arms that embrace,
For love that is given comes back round and round again.
May these rings (extend them in the palm of your hand)
Remind you that your love,
Like the sun shines brightly,
That your love,
Like the eye sees clearly,
And that your love,
Like arms that embrace,
Truly is a gift to our world.

Intro: After reading this passage, hold out the rings to the couple and say something like: "When you look on these rings, may you be filled with courage and joy." Then you hand the groom the ring he's giving to his bride, and have him repeat after you, one of the versions of the Ring Exchange listed in the next section. With a same-sex couple, I suggest that the person who offered their vows second be the person to offer the ring first.

#3

These are the hands of your best friend, young, strong and full of love for you.
These are the hands that will work alongside yours, as together you build your future.
These are the hands that will passionately cherish you through the years,
And with the slightest touch, will comfort you like no other.
These are the hands that will hold you when fear or grief fills your mind.
That will wipe away countless tears—tears of joy and of sorrow.
These are the hands that will tenderly hold your family as one.
And these are the hands that, even when aged, will still reach out to you with the same touch that comforts you this day.

Intro: After reading this passage, hold out the rings to the couple and say something like: "Whenever you glance on these rings, know that you are loved beyond all imagining." Then you hand the groom the ring he's giving to his bride, and have him repeat after you, one of the versions of the Ring Exchange listed in the next section. With a same-sex couple, I suggest that the person who offered their vows second be the person to offer the ring first.

#4

The book of love is long and boring.
No one can lift the damn thing,
It's full of charts and facts and figures
And instructions for dancing.

But, I, I love it when you read to me,
And you, you can read me anything.

The book of love is long and boring
And written very long ago.
It's full of flowers and heart-shaped boxes,
And things we're all too young to know.

But, I, I love it when you give me things
And you, you ought to give me wedding rings.

I, I love it when you give me things
And you, you ought to give me wedding rings.

~Stephen Merritt
The Book of Love

Intro: After reading this passage, hold out the rings to the couple and say something like: "May these rings always inspire you to live a life that is anything but boring!" Then you hand the groom the ring he's giving to his bride, and have him repeat after you, one of the versions of the Ring Exchange listed below. With a same-sex couple, I suggest that the person who offered their vows second be the person to offer the ring first.

Bonus # 9

Words For The Exchange Of Rings

After reading one of the above Intro passages, or another passage of the couple's choosing, you then hand the groom the ring he's giving to his bride and ask him to repeat after you some version of the following. After the ring is on the bride's finger, you hand her the ring she's giving to her groom and repeat. With a same-sex couple, I suggest that the person who offered their vows second be the person to offer the ring first.

You whisper to the groom (and later to the bride): "As you place this ring on N's finger, please repeat after me:"

A.
I give you this ring as a symbol of my vows, and, with all that I am and all that I have, I honor you.

B.
I give you this ring as a pledge of my love, as the symbol of our unity.

C.
With this ring, I thee wed.

D.
With this ring, as a pledge of my love, I join my life with yours in faithful kindness and compassion.

E.
With all that I am and all that I have, I give you this ring as a symbol of my love.

F.
You are my lover, my best friend—all times, all places, all ways, forever.

Bonus #10

Unity Candle Readings

#1.

True love is a sacred flame
That burns eternally,
And none can dim its special glow
Or change that destiny.
True love speaks in tender tones
And hears with gentle ear,
True love gives with open heart
And true love conquers fear.
True love makes no harsh demands
It neither rules nor binds,
And true love holds with gentle hands
The hearts that it entwines.
For true love is a sacred flame
That burns eternally.

#2.

From every human being there rises a light that reaches straight to
heaven. And when two souls that are destined to be together find each
other, their streams of light flow together and a single, brighter light
goes forth from their united being.

#3.

Soft mists embrace two golden flames,
Alone they search the night.
Two souls adrift in dreams of love,
They seek to claim the light.
The path is long from which they came,
But sure they are it's right.
Two flames embrace in dreams of love,
Two souls—two hearts unite.

By Harold Douglas

Bonus #11

Final Blessings

#1

May God bless you and guide you in your faithful commitment to one another.
May God defend you and shelter you in your tender love for one another.
May God uphold you in all life's challenges and shower you with all life's rewards,
So that you always find strength and delight in each other
And so grow in love until your life's end. AMEN.

#2

May God bless you and keep you.
May God's countenance shine upon you
And be gracious to you.
May God give you peace:
Peace in your hearts,
Peace in your home,
Peace in your united lives,
Indeed, peace unto eternity.

#3

Good and faithful God, we thank you for the love and joy N & N have found in each other. Pour down your grace that they may fulfill the vows they have made this day and reflect your steadfast love in their faithfulness to each other. May they continue to grow in wisdom, understanding, patience, respect, affection, and love towards you, towards each other, and toward your world in all its richness and diversity. Dear God, in your graciousness, use all of us here present to support them in their promises and life together. AMEN.

#4

Now, as you go forth from this place to live out your lives, we pray that the abundant blessings of God, your family and friends may keep you together always in true understanding, honest tenderness and courageous love all the days of your life!

#5

Loving God, our hearts are filled with gratitude on this N and N's wedding day. In hope and confidence, we ask you to grant that they may be ever true and loving, living together in such a way as to never bring heartache into their marriage. Ignite their hearts with kindness and help them to be helpmates, friend and guide so that together they may meet the cares and problems of life bravely and wisely. Let them never take each other for granted, finding contentment in the riches of companionship. May their home be a place of harmony where your spirit shines. Walk beside them all their life together. And may their love continue unto life eternal. AMEN.

#6

May the road rise to meet you.
May the wind be always at your back.
May the sun shine warm upon your face,
The rains soft upon the fields.

May the light of friendship guide your paths together.
May the laughter of children grace the halls of your home.
May the joy of living for one another trip a smile from your lips,
And a twinkle from your eye.

And when eternity beckons
At the end of a life heaped high with love,
May the good Lord embrace you
With the arms that have nurtured you
The whole length of your joy-filled days.

May the Spirit of Love
Find a dwelling place in your hearts
Today, tomorrow, and always.

#7

Loving God, source of life's blessings, we humbly pray to you for N & N, who today are united in marriage. May your fullest blessing come upon them so that they may together rejoice in your gift of love. Lord, may they both praise you when they are happy and turn to you in their sorrows. May they be glad that you help them in their work and know that you are with them in need. May they pray to you in the community of their family and friends and be reflections of your graciousness in our world. May they reach old age in the company of their friends and come at last to the kingdom of heaven. AMEN.

#8

May the road rise to meet you.
May the wind be always at your back.

May the warm rays of sun fall upon your home
And may the hand of a friend always be near.

May green be the grass you walk on,
May blue be the skies above you.

May pure be the joys that surround you,
May true be the hearts that love you.

May you see your children's children.
May you be poor in misfortune,
Rich in blessings.

May you know nothing but happiness
From this day forward.

May the sun shine warm upon your face,
The rains fall soft upon your fields.

And until we meet again,
May God be with you and bless you.

#9

This blessing could be offered by you OR six different people could offer the blessing

Officiant: Dear God, we thank you for N & N and the gift of their love in our lives. With grateful hearts, we pray:

a.   Bless them so that each may be to the other, a strength in need, a helper in perplexity, a comfort in sorrow, and a companion in joy.

b.   Grant that their own lives will be so united with yours, dear God, that they may grow in love and peace with you and one another all the days of their lives.

c.   Grant them grace when they hurt each other, to recognize and acknowledge their fault, and to seek each other's forgiveness and yours.

d.   Make their life together a sign of your love to our world, oh God, so that unity may overcome separation, forgiveness heal guilt, and joy conquer despair.

e.   Give them joy and hope in their mutual affection so that they may reach out in love and concern to others.

f.   Grant that we, who have witnessed their vows, may find our own lives strengthened and renewed in faith and hope.

Officiant: We thank you, dear God, for hearing our prayers and we ask that you answer these prayers in your own good way, in your own good time, allowing each of us to be a part of your answer. With faith, hope, and love we open our hearts (in the name of Jesus, your beloved, our lord and brother). AMEN.

Bonus #12

Non-Religious Words Of Sending Forth

#1

Here all seeking is over, the lost has been found,
A mate has been found
To share the chills of winter.
Now love asks that you be united.
Here is a place to rest,
A place to sleep,
A place in heaven.
Now two are becoming one,
For the black night is scattered,
The eastern sky grows bright.
At last the great day has come.

#2

May the blessing of light be with you always;
Light without and light within.
May the sun shine upon you
And warm your hearts
Until they glow like a great fire,
So that all who know you
May feel the warmth of your love for each other.

#3

May you work like you don't need the money.
May you love you've never been hurt.
May you dance like nobody is watching.

And may you preserve in each other
A passionate zest for the world,
Much gentleness,
And always help each other be ever more fully human.

#4

Now you will feel no rain,
For each of you will be a shelter for the other.
Now you will feel no cold,
For each of you will be warmth to the other.

Now there will be no loneliness,
For each of you will be companion to the other.

May beauty surround you in the journey,
May happiness be your companion and
May your days together be good and long upon the earth.
Treat yourselves and each other with respect, and
Give to tenderness and kindness the highest priority.

When frustration and fear assail your relationship,
Focus on what is right between you,
Not on what seems wrong.

Take responsibility for the quality of your life together,
So it will be marked by abundance and delight.

Live knowing that now you are two persons, but
There is only one life before you.

#5

Now it is completed,
The marriage ceremony,
Just like the moon descending
In its drizzling radiance.
The couple is given the happiness
Of those who watch,
Which showers down upon them like gold.
This is the symbol,
The marriage ceremony,
With the blessings of all the guests,
That this marriage may be free from all misfortune
And bear eternal happiness forever.

~Javanese poem

#6

Rejoicing in the promise of this moment,
In the giving and receiving of your hearts to each other,
We now bid you both:

May you share in each other's joys and sorrows,
Achievements and dreams.

May sensitivity and understanding deepen,
While you nurture one another through growth and challenge.

May you respect and strengthen each other's individuality,
As you hold precious the truth of this union.

May patience and understanding be yours to call upon,
With forgiveness as your ready and trusty expression of love.

And so may you create a home that places love, kindness and compassion
Into the hearts of your families friends, as well as your own,
Today, tomorrow, and always.

#7

May you comfort and encourage each other as
Sharers of each others dreams,
Conscience of each others sorrows,
Helpers to each other in all life's challenges.

May you cheer on each other in whatever you set out to achieve.
May you trust each other, as you trust life unafraid.

May you offer wisdom and support to all who seek your recognition.
May you create a life rooted in patience, tolerance and understanding.

And may you receive all the exquisite excitements,
Expected and unexpected, that a marriage embraced must bring.

#8

Scattered from hands of love like bread for birds,
Flung like rainbows of confetti from hands of joy,
We shower you with blessings!

May happiness be the bricks that build your house.
May compassion be the roof that shelters you.
May respect be the windows that offer you light.
May gladness be the table that welcomes friends and family.

May courage sustain you,
With love as your guide.

May life be long and at its human end,
May the gaze that falls each upon the other
Be still alive with tenderness,
And twinkle yet with laughter.

With grateful hearts we celebrate
Your wedding day!

Bonus #13

Words For When You Pronounce The Couple Married

After you have offered the couple a Final Blessing or a Sending Forth, you then pronounce them married and introduce them ala, "Mr. & Mrs. Jack & Jill Smith." You can also pronounce and present them at the same time. Here are versions of how you can word all this:

#1

"N & N, you have expressed your love to one another through the commitment and promises you have made here today. With these in mind, I now pronounce that you are husband and wife. Now you may kiss."

Step aside so photographer can get snap of first kiss without you in the background! After the kiss, step back and say something to the effect,

"Family and friends, I present to you Mr. & Mrs. Jack & Jill Smith." Strike up music. Begin Recessional.

OR

"N & N, you have expressed your love to one another through the commitment and promises you have made here today. With these in mind and by the authority vested in me, I now pronounce as and present for the first time as husband and wife, Mr. & Mrs. Jack & Jill Smith."

Step aside so photographer can get snap of first kiss without you in the background! Strike up music. Begin Recessional.

#2

"Since you have consented to join together in the bond of matrimony, and have pledged yourselves to each other in the presence of these loving friends, I now pronounce you partners in marriage."

Step aside so photographer can get snap of first kiss without you in the background! After the kiss, step back and say something to the effect, "Family and friends, I present to you Mr. & Mrs. Jack & Jill Smith."

Strike up music. Begin Recessional.

OR

"Since N&N have consented to join together in the bond of matrimony, and have pledged themselves to each other in the presence of you, their loving friends, by the power vested in me, I now pronounce as and present for the first time as partners in marriage, Mr. & Mrs. Jack & Jill Smith."

Step aside so photographer can get snap of first kiss without you in the background! Strike up music. Begin Recessional.

#3

"Forasmuch as N & N have pledged their love and loyalty to each other, and have declared the same by the joining and the giving of rings, by the power vested in me, and as witnessed by friends and family, I now pronounce you husband and wife."

Step aside so photographer can get snap of first kiss without you in the background! After the kiss, step back and say something to the effect, "Family and friends, I present to you Mr. & Mrs. Jack & Jill Smith."

Strike up music. Begin Recessional.

OR

"Forasmuch as N & N have pledged their love and loyalty to each other, and have declared the same by the joining and the giving of rings, by the power vested in me, and as witnessed by friends and family, I now pronounce as and present for the first time as husband and wife, Mr. & Mrs. Jack & Jill Smith."

Step aside so photographer can get snap of first kiss without you in the background! Strike up music. Begin Recessional.

Bonus #14

Romantic Quotes To Inspire You

In a marriage, you're promising to care about everything. The good things, the bad things, the terrible things, the mundane things—all of it, all of the time, every day. You're saying, 'your life will not go unnoticed because I will notice it.' Your life will not go un-witnessed because I will be your witness.'

From the movie, Shall We Dance?

In that book which is my memory, on the first page of the chapter that is the day when I first met you, appear the words: 'here begins a new life.'

Dante

Without words, without even understanding, lovers find each other. The moment of finding is always a surprise, like meeting an old friend never before known.

Lao Tzu

To love someone deeply gives you strength. Being loved by someone deeply gives you courage.

Lao Tzu

Love has nothing to do with what you are expecting to get, only with what you are expecting to give – which is everything.

Katherine Hepburn

Love doesn't sit there like a stone, it has to be made, like bread; remade all of the time, made new.

Ursula LeGuin

Anyone can be passionate, but it takes real lovers to be silly.

Rose Franken

You have made a place in my heart where I thought there was no room for anything else. You have made flowers grow where I cultivated dust and stones.

Robert Jordan

We are all a little weird and life's a little weird, and when we find someone whose weirdness is compatible with ours, we join up with them and fall in mutual weirdness and call it love.

Robert Fulghum

Married couples who love each other tell each other a thousand things without talking.

Chinese Proverb

The one word above all others that makes marriage successful is "ours."

Robert Quillem

The goal of our life should not be to find joy in marriage, but to bring more love and truth into the world. We marry to assist each other in this task.

Leo Tolstoy

Love consists in this: that two solitudes protect and touch and greet each other.

Rilke

The first duty of love is to listen.

Tillich

A happy marriage is a long conversation that always seems too short.

Andre Malroux

I want to do with you what spring does with the cherry trees.

Pablo Neruda

I want to say: all my life I was a bride married to amazement. I was a bridegroom, taking the world into my arms.

Mary Oliver

Never love anyone who treats you as ordinary.

Oscar Wilde

Love is being stupid together.

Paul Valery

Two people fall in love, and decide to see if their love might stand up over time, if there might be enough grace and forgiveness and memory lapses to help the whole shebang hang together.

Anne Lamott

For it was not into my ear you whispered, but into my heart. It was not my lips you kissed, but my soul.

Judy Garland

How shall we know ourselves, except in the clarifying mirror of some other gaze?

Mark Doty

Love, I think, is a gateway to the world, not an escape from it.

Mark Doty

From this day forward, you shall not walk alone. My heart will be your shelter, and my arms will be your home.

Marianne Williamson

The very least you can do in your life is to figure out what you hope for.

Barbara Kingsolver

My whole life changed when I decided not just what I'd like to do, but when I decided who I was committed to being and having in my life.

Tony Robbins

Life is not measured by the number of breaths we take, but by the moments that take our breath away.

George Carlin

Love is our true destiny. We do not find the meaning of life by ourselves alone – we find it in another. The meaning of our life is a secret that has to be revealed to us in love, by the one we love. The one who loves is more alive and more real than when they did not love.

Thomas Merton

My life can be measured by the moments I've had with you.

Joan Fontaine

When we talked, I felt brilliant, fascinating; she brought out the version of myself I like most.

Nadir Alsadir

The greatest thing you'll ever learn is to love and be loved in return.

Moulin Rouge

The best way to know life is to love many things.

Van Gogh

But in love, something miraculous happens. In loving someone, we give them an ideal against which to measure themselves. Living in the presence of that ideal, the beloved strives to fulfill the lover's expectations. In this way, love makes of us the bravest and best persons that we are capable of being.

Fenton Johnson

A good relationship is based on unconditional love. It's not some maudlin feeling – it's a decision. The mature relationship image I like best is two people making music together. Each plays his/her own instrument and uses his/her own unique skills, but they play the same song. Each is whole and complete. Each is independent and committed.

John Bradshaw

If love could be grown in every field across the land, would we value it as highly? It is rare and precious and has to be found buried in the hard rocks of daily life. Life is long and the struggle fierce, so many things will conspire to pull you apart, so many crises for which there seem to be no rules.

Unknown

Music I heard with you was more than music and bread I broke with you was more than break.

Conrad Aiken

In this world without pity, when all the answers, they don't amount to much, you just want someone to hold onto, you need a little of the human touch.

Bruce Springsteen

Make yourself necessary to someone.

Emerson

To fall in love is easy, but it is a hard quest worth making, to find a comrade through whose steady presence one becomes the person one desires to be.

Anna Louise Strong

We come to love not by finding a perfect person, but by learning to see an imperfect person perfectly.

Sam Keen

NEW BONUS #15

The Question Couples Most Often Ask

The question I get asked most often by couples is this: "Is it okay if we – ?" And that blank is filled in with a wildly imaginative assortment of ideas. Thumb through contemporary wedding planning books and you'll notice that tradition is adapting to many modern inclinations. I officiated a wedding where the bride had a "man-of-honor" and the groom had a "best woman." Another bride, whose parents were deceased, had her pot-bellied pig "escort" her down the aisle. A shy groom, who was a musician, wrote a song for his bride and sang it in place of "saying" his own vows.

A few memories that still make me smile ~
• The bride who walked down the aisle to the blaring of the Star Wars theme. Yes, it did have an other-worldly feel to it.
• The bride who did somersaults down the aisle (she was in her 40's). More than being stunned, I was amazed that she could do them while wearing an evening dress.
• The bride who planned her wedding, guided by her astrological chart. She determined that the vows had to be said beginning exactly at 5:59 PM. I had a friend stand off to the comer and flag me when it was time.
• And then there was the couple that had their wedding in the backyard of their new home. As a symbol of their pledge to wholeheartedly "take the plunge" they jumped into the pool after I pronounced them married.

I really haven't seen it all, but I've seen enough to know that the whacky and unexpected sometimes can add to the sweetness of the day. And the day is all about sweet, poignant, moments and touches. Some can be planned for and many cannot.

true story ~

I officiated a wedding in a chapel built on the grounds of a retirement home. The bride's great-grandfather had built the chapel. It was there that he himself officiated the wedding of Emily's grandparents. It was here that her parents got married. Tradition and family made this space especially sacred.

Emily and Adam were glowing as they stood before me, ever present to the moment. And then, as I was introducing the Exchange Of Vows, Emily spotted something on Adam's jacket. Instinctively, she reached across and flicked it away. Everyone laughed, though the couple seemed clueless to our reaction.

It was an exquisite moment. That one gesture spoke to the reality of marriage – caring in simple ways – reaching gently across to help each other. The visual captured the moment in a way words never could.

That's why a wedding ceremony has the power to renew and refresh by grounding us in what life is all about – friends, family, love, loyalty – and by reminding us of who we are and who we are meant to be. And for twenty minutes YOU are the host of all this magic!

NEW BONUS #16

Interviews With Two 1st-Time Officiants

Since the time this book was first published, I've coached scores of people in how to create ceremonies that reflect their couple as well as reflect their own style of speaking.

Anthony and Ray are two of the many people I've coached. They were quick learners – as well as they should be since I had officiated each of their weddings more than twenty years ago! Anthony and his wife, Melissa, along with Ray and his wife, Stephanie, are good friends of mine.

Anthony and Ray were each asked to officiate a relative's wedding (Anthony actually ended up officiating three weddings this year). These guys are smart, funny and articulate and each is comfortable speaking in a professional setting. Each, though, was frantic as they realized they didn't understand what went into making a wedding ceremony!

Anthony and Ray each worked diligently with me on their respective outlines and scripts and each was glowing after officiating his first wedding. Since they had a super positive experience I interviewed each via a brief questionnaire. I think you'll find their answers both reassuring and informative!

Anthony C.

How many ceremonies have you officiated?

Three ceremonies

What is your relationship to the couple(s)?

(1) Friend and landlord (akin to asking the ship's captain to marry you, I guess)

(2) Elder brother

(3) Cousin by marriage

What was your first reaction when the couple asked you to officiate their wedding?

A. Nervousness, panic - a feeling of being found out as a fraud – concerned that I not ruin this couple's wedding day.

What were you most nervous or worried about as you prepared for the ceremony?

A. I was most worried that I wasn't going to be able to sufficiently capture the sentiments of the couple and of the audience in my prepared remarks. I was also concerned about how to handle all of the technical issues (the cameras recording the event and where I should stand to be out of the way of the photo op, handling the mics, do I hold the mic or hand off to the couple when they say their vows?

Did any of your fears come true and if so how did you manage them?

A. None whatsoever. Your book prepared me well for the event.

What did your couple most enjoy or appreciate about the ceremony?

A. The couple and extended family and friends most appreciated that my service supported their uniqueness as a couple. I think the groom's mother initially had her doubts. About 30 minutes before the ceremony she gave me a gentle lecture about who these two were as a couple and how they did things. I think she was worried that I would be a control freak and impose my will and my ideas on the couple's ceremony.

Is there anything you wish you had done differently?

A. Honestly? No - it was a perfect first wedding.

Were there any mishaps? If so, how did you handle them?

A. The camera crew had the microphone in an odd place that would have put us too far under the awning and cramped the couple. I asked the crew to attach the mic to the edge of the overhang. I made the decision that, given the choice between staging that looks good for the camera, and staging that serves the live event and the couple and attendees - the live event would have to prevail.

What was the most challenging aspect of officiating the ceremony?

A. It was a very small space. The couple wanted to get married in a building in a faux
Western Town with a very small porch. I had to move them off the porch so that they
could be better seen and appreciated by their family and friends.

What did you most enjoy about the experience of officiating?

A. I most enjoyed listening to my couple in our planning conversations, finding out what THEY wanted (i.e. - what was the movie that played in their heads as they imagined their wedding day), and working to deliver an experience that supported and reflected who they are as a couple.

What advice would you give to someone reading this book and who will soon officiate their first ceremony?

A. Remember that this day is all about the couple - and that you are there to support THEM. If you approach the ceremony with the perspective of, "How can I help this couple celebrate their love and commitment to each other in a way that truly reflects who they are?" you take your focus and potential stage fright off of you and place your attention on your couple.

I would also say to expect and welcome the unexpected - make the mistakes and accidents and hiccups part of the celebration. Acknowledge them with good humor and move on - fun and smiles are infectious.

Would you officiate another ceremony?

A. Yes.

Ray Y.

How many ceremonies have you officiated?

A. Just one so far!

What is your relationship to the couple(s)?

A. I am a cousin (and honorary uncle) to the bride.

What was your first reaction when the couple asked you to officiate their wedding?

A. I was at first surprised at the request (as I had never done this before) and then I was really touched that they thought enough of me to ask (they were not connected to another faith community and were not sure where to go to get a personal ceremony). I suppose they were not comfortable asking someone they did not know to lead a ceremony that is so personal.

What were you most nervous or worried about while preparing the ceremony?

A. During prep, I was most concerned with two things. 1) Having an appropriate story to tell in the "words of good cheer" and 2) making sure that the structure of the ceremony would be fluid and provide for a true sense of ceremony.

Did any of your fears come true and if so how did you manage them?

A. I must admit that the ceremony went very well and most of my fears did not materialize! Although I was afraid that no one could see me as I am on the shorter side and the couple (and their wedding party) were all on the very tall side. Other than that all went according to plan. And speaking of plan, that is the real key, planning. I followed the step-by-step ceremony guide outlined in this book and that was the key; along with practicing many times.

What did your couple most appreciate about the ceremony?

A. One of the funny things (to me) was that the bride loved the story I told during the "words of good cheer," which was the part I was most nervous about! I also know they really loved the fact that I was connected to them and helped to connect all the guests to the bride and groom.

Is there anything you wish you had done differently?

A. I wish I had remembered to tell the guests to sit down after the opening remarks! Other than that, the wine box ritual was staged a bit clumsily, but mainly due to the fact there was very little room to move at the venue as it was a small courtyard.

Were there any mishaps? How did you handle them?

A. My main "mishap" was the fact that I did not ask the guests to sit after the welcome. And since I could not see the guests too well I did not notice. At the wine ceremony the photographer came up to me and said I might ask the guests to sit! I handled it by explaining that the bride and groom were so tall I could not see the guests standing and once they moved away I noticed their discomfort – a few chuckles were produced. However, some people still stood even after the invitation to sit.

What was the most challenging aspect of officiating the ceremony?

A. The preparation was the most challenging aspect for me. Since in the professional world I give presentations to groups of all sizes, I was not concerned about the delivery, but more concerned about the content. I needed to get to the point where I understood that I did have good words to say. The content was atypical for me, but following the guidelines really helped me to break down the steps and allowed me to focus on the actual words of content.

What did you most enjoy about the experience of officiating?

A. Odd to say, but what I enjoyed most was the fact that being known to half of the guests gave the ceremony a relaxed feel and helped the ceremony feel more personal to me as the officiant. During the ceremony I also enjoyed the sheer emotion of the bride and groom during the vows and exchange of rings. The groom was so emotional at one point that I think my voice may have cracked due to the emotion!

What advice would you give to someone reading this book and who will soon officiate their first ceremony?

A. The best advice I can give is to understand that your role as the officiant is to bring the bride and groom and their guests through a joyful occasion, it is not a time to be preachy. Also, follow the steps in the book as to the form of the ceremony itself. Breaking down the steps according to the book really helped me to build the content within each segment. Also, once your first draft is done, try to be aware of the wording. I worked with JP Reynolds and one of the points he brought to light was that my words were very formal and not how I would normally speak.

Would you officiate another ceremony?

A. I would definitely officiate again! In fact, I have already been asked to do another wedding by a cousin who was present at this ceremony. Once I got through the first ceremony, the second does not seem as daunting.

A 1st Time Officiant's Script – Before and After

This is the 1st draft that my friend Ray wrote. My initial suggestions are in italics. He had good instincts and he also made some common missteps!

1st DRAFT

Words Of Welcome:

Good evening and welcome to the event of the summer!

Actually, your first words should be: "My name is Ray Y and on behalf of Janet and Charles I welcome you to their wedding celebration – to THE event of the summer! Please be seated."

Because not everyone knows who you are, you need to introduce yourself. You are welcoming everyone on behalf of the couple. Also, remember – if you do not tell people to sit, they may not sit down!

Janet, Charles, we meet here today, at this time and place to make public what you both have begun. We are here to witness and bless your love for each other and your choice to be bound to each other in front of your friends and family.

Nice, but – it sounds stiff and formal. Establish your credentials – tell guests what your relationship is to the couple. Reference how you're feeling, i.e. your joy at being asked to officiate and then remind the couple that looking out you can see that you're not the only person happy to be with them.

Please, Janet and Charles, turn and take a look at all of your guests gathered here today in your honor to witness and embrace your gift of love.

To all gathered here today *(why so formal?)* whether you realize it or not, you are the reason that Charles and Janet are here and committed to love each other. Love is learned and love is witnessed. Without the love and commitment of family and friends, Janet and Charles might never have been able to choose each other.

As we begin our ceremony it is good to recall that laced through our celebration today is the abiding love of those who have gone before us. Know that they are here and present with us today.

Opening Prayer:
Let us pray.

A bit abrupt – I'd say something like, "On this day of thanksgiving, let us with grateful hearts pray for Janet and Charles. PAUSE. Then, 'Let us pray'."

Good and faithful God, we thank you for this great day! We thank you for the gift of Janet and Charles, for the gift of their love in our lives. Bless us all; bless our celebration and through what we do here today, may we become the reflection of your compassion and graciousness in our world. We ask this of You with hearts filled with faith, hope and love. In the name of Jesus our brother – Amen!

Words Of Good Cheer:

I remember a story of a couple that were married a very long time. Both living into their late '80's. The husband was a shoe salesman at Sears Roebuck Company and for their wedding day he purchased a pair of black patent leather dress shoes to wear with his tuxedo. While he was very stylish for the wedding day, he continued to wear the special shoes each year on their wedding anniversary. Annually he removed them from their box, gave them a brief wipe with a cloth and placed them on his feet to celebrate the day he was joined to his life love. This simple gesture and simple article of clothing over the years came to symbolize not only the great day of their commitment to each other, but also an outward sign of their continued celebration of the love they shared. Simple – a pair of shoes, elegant – they were patent leather shoes after all, symbolic – a sign of celebration.

Charles, Janet – today begins a great new chapter in the story of your lives, and as you write your pages remember to look for the simple, elegant and symbolic gifts within your new life together as these are precious.

Ray had good instincts here since Charles actually likes shoes and has quite a collection. So, Ray has a good story. The "Words Of Good Cheer" is a moment when you, the officiant, can offer an "official" wish on behalf of all present. After all, this is a day of wishing and hoping. Where Ray goes astray is towards the end, in the section I bold-faced. He's turning this story into a lecture as he starts to talk about the symbolism of the shoes. You don't have to go in that direction. From the story, you want to make a wish. So, I suggested something along the lines of, "Charles, even though the shoes you're wearing today aren't patent-leather (said in light-hearted tone of voice), my wish is that in the years to come you both always celebrate the little moments of your life together and that you care for each other with as much detail as though every day were an anniversary."

Exchange Of Vows:

If you would please turn and face each other and Charles, take Janet's hands in yours.

NO! You don't need to give stage directions out loud. Whisper this to them without the mic.

Marriage begins in the giving of your word. You cannot join yourselves to one another without giving your word. This must be unconditional, for in joining yourselves to each other, you are joining yourselves to tomorrow, the unknown and ever-changing surprise of life.

Charles, repeat after me.

Too abrupt – you need to reference that the guests are prepared to witness the giving of your vows. Say something like, "And so we who are your family and friends gratefully bear witness as you make your vow to each other." Also, You don't need to tell them to repeat after you – just nod and point the mic in the person's direction.

I, Charles take you Janet to be my wife – To have and to hold from this day forward – For better, for worse – For richer, for poorer – In sickness and in health – To love and to cherish until death do us part.
Janet, repeat after me.

I, Janet take you Charles to be my husband – To have and to hold from this day forward – For better, for worse – For richer, for poorer – In sickness and in health – To love and to cherish until death do us part.

I remind you that God abundantly blesses your love and whom God has joined let no one divide!

This is a great classic line used in ceremonies with religious overtones. It needs to be delivered with a punch, so I'd say, "Charles, Janet, you have pledged your word and your life to each other and I remind you that God. . ."

Exchange Of Rings:

In ancient times, it was believed that the vein on the fourth finger of the left hand led directly to the heart. Please bring forward the rings.

"These are the hands of your best friend, young, strong and full of love for you. These are the hands that will work alongside yours, as together you build your future. These are the hands that will passionately cherish you through the years, and with the slightest touch, will comfort you like no other. These are the hands that will tenderly hold your family as one. And these are the hands that will tenderly hold your family as one. And these are the hands that, even when aged, will still reach out to you with the same touch that comforts you this day."

"Whenever you glance at these rings, know that you are loved beyond all imagining."

All of this is solid but it needs to be delivered correctly. I suggested to Ray that he first ask for the rings saying, "I now ask for the presentation of the rings." The rings are given to Ray. Then he should look at the couple and say, "In ancient times, it was believed that the vein on the fourth finger of the left hand led directly to the heart. Janet, Charles, I invite you to join hands." Once they are holding hands, he would say, "These are the hands. . ."

Charles, as you place this ring on Janet's finger, repeat after me –
"I give you this ring as a pledge of my love and the symbol of our unity."

Janet, repeat after me _
"I give you this ring as a pledge of my love and the symbol of our unity."

No need to say out loud the above words – just whisper to the person.

Final Blessing:

Thank you Janet and Charles for the gift that this day is to all of us. Your love has brought us all together on this day, at this time, in this place.

Before you say anything, look out at the guests, smile and say, "Please stand." Then say the above.

Charles, Janet, as you go forth from this place to live out your lives, know that we pray that the abundant blessings of God, your family and friends may keep you together always in true understanding, honest tenderness and courageous love all the days of your life!

Pronouncement and Presentation:

"And now" – PAUSE –
By the power vested in me, it is my honor to pronounce as, and to present for the first time as husband and wife – Mr. and Mrs. Christopher Jones – PAUSE – Now you may kiss!

REMEMBER! Step aside as soon as you say "Now you may kiss."

FINAL DRAFT

Here is the final script Ray wrote and delivered in the ceremony. You'll see how he tightened-up the wording and overall flow. The couple also decided that they wanted to incorporate the Wine Box Ritual, which had not been in the original draft.

You'll also notice that in this final draft Ray forgot to invite the guests to be seated. As it turns out, most of them remained standing throughout the ceremony! Remember – you are the host and conductor of the ceremony and people will take their cues from you.

+++

Words of Welcome:

Good evening! I am Ray Yancer, also known as Uncle Ray, and I am thrilled to have been asked to officiate at this wonderful event! I would like to welcome everyone to the family event of the summer!

Janet and Charles, take a moment to turn and take a look at all of your guests gathered here today in your honor to witness and embrace your gift of love.

Family, Friends – whether you realize it or not, you are a large part of the reason that Charles and Janet are here and committed to love each other. Love is learned and love is witnessed. Without the love and commitment of all of you, Janet and Charles might never have been able to choose each other.

And as we enter into our ceremony, it is good to recall that laced through our celebration today is the abiding love of those who have gone before us. Those special people that have been with us in our lives – they are here and present with us today.

Opening Prayer:

And so, with much gratitude, Let us pray ~
Good and faithful God, we thank you for this great day! We thank you for the gift of Janet and Charles, for the gift of their love in our lives. Bless us all; bless our celebration and through what we do here today, may we become the reflection of your compassion and graciousness in our world. We ask this of you with hearts filled with faith, hope and love. In the name of Jesus, Amen!

Words of Good Cheer:

Weddings are a time of good cheer, filled with storytelling and good wishes. I am sure that at the reception there will be an abundance of stories about Janet and Charles that will both amuse and perhaps make them blush!

As I was thinking about today, I was reminded of an elderly couple we knew. Harry and Dorothy were married for a very long time and both lived together into their late 80's. Harry had worked as a shoe salesman at Sears Roebuck Company and that is where he met his future wife, Dorothy.

For their wedding day, Harry purchased a pair of black patent leather dress shoes to wear with his suit. While very stylish for the time, those shoes would become a ritual of remembrance of their happy day. Every year on their anniversary, Harry would bring down the worn box containing the shoes, gently wipe them with a cloth to return their luster and then place them on his feet to celebrate the day he was joined to his life's love.

While this may seem curious to the outside world, this simple ritual of wearing his patent leather wedding shoes was a reminder of that special day and a celebration of the love they shared.

My wish for the two of you is not just to always have a closet filled with shoes (!), but that you always celebrate the loving details of life. That you cherish and seek out the small acts of love that manifest themselves in how you care for each other.

Charles, Janet, today begins a great new chapter in the story of your lives, and as you write your pages, remember to look for the simple and elegant gifts within your new life together – as these are precious and will last a lifetime.

Exchange of Vows:

Marriage begins in the giving of your word. You cannot join yourselves to one another without giving your word. This must be unconditional, for in joining yourselves to each other, you are joining yourselves to tomorrow – to the unknown and ever-changing surprise of life.
Charles, repeat after me (whispered)

I, Charles take you Janet to be my wife. To have and to hold from this day forward. For better, for worse. For richer, for poorer. In sickness and in health. To love and to cherish until death do us part.

Janet, repeat after me (whispered)

I, Janet take you Charles to be my husband. To have and to hold from this day forward. For better, for worse. For richer, for poorer. In sickness and in health. To love and to cherish until death do us part.

Charles and Janet, you have spoken from your hearts and pledged your vows to each other and so I remind you that God abundantly blesses your love – AND whom God has joined – let no one divide!

Exchange of Rings:

Please bring forward the rings.

In ancient times, it was believed that the vein on the fourth finger of the left hand led directly to the heart – and thus, the "ring finger."

Charles, Janet, I remind you that – These are the hands of your best friend, young, strong and full of love for you. These are the hands that will work alongside yours, as together you build your future. These are the hands that will passionately cherish you through the years, and with the slightest touch, will comfort you like no other. These are the hands that will tenderly hold your family as one. And these are the hands that, even when aged, will still reach out to you with the same touch that comforts you this day.

Holding the rings:

Whenever you glance at these rings, know that you are loved beyond all imagining.

Charles, as you place this ring on Janet's finger, repeat after me (whispered)

I give you this ring as a pledge of my love and the symbol of our unity.

Janet repeat after me (whispered)

I give you this ring—as a pledge of my love and the symbol of our unity.

Wine Box Ritual:

A wise person once said, "Wine is constant proof that God loves us and loves to see us happy."

To continue to celebrate this happy occasion, Janet and Charles have picked a special bottle of wine. They have also written letters to each other that will now be placed in the box with the wine. If you have not written your wishes for them, this wine box will be here throughout the evening for each of you to write a note expressing a wish, happy thought or prayer for Janet and Charles.

On their first anniversary they will open this box, share the wine, and read the letters and notes from this happy day. And trust me, the wine will taste better and be more satisfying than the top of their wedding cake!

Final Blessing:

This is a great day! On behalf of myself and everyone gathered here today, I want to thank you, Janet and Charles, for the gift that this day is to all of us. May you always find in each other the love, laughter and happiness that only partners in life can share!

And so ~ As you go forth from this place to live out your lives, we pray that the abundant blessings of God, your family and friends may keep you together always in true understanding, honest tenderness and courageous love all the days of your life!

Pronouncement and Presentation:

And now! By the power vested in me, it is my honor to pronounce as, and to present for the first time as husband and wife – "Mr. and Mrs. Charles Bonner." Now you may kiss!

NEW BONUS #18

How To Personalize A Ceremony Incorporating
Family and Friends

One night, when I was a freshman in college, I paid my grandmother a surprise visit. When I was leaving, she slipped into my hand a twenty-dollar bill and gave me a tight hug and a big kiss. I squirmed. I was eighteen and too old for all that mushy stuff – but I did appreciate the money! She squeezed tighter and whispered, "You'll never know how much I love you."

Now, all these years later, I'm a wedding officiant and almost every weekend I stand before a couple and bear witness to their vows. And each time, as I look out on the gathering of family and friends, I realize that the couple before me will probably never know just how much they are loved.

For me, a wedding ceremony is a HUGE hug that family and friends offer to the couple. Yes, at its core, the ceremony honors and celebrates the love and commitment of the couple. BUT, the ceremony is also that unique time to celebrate all the loves that have helped to bring a couple to that moment in time – parents and grandparents, aunts and uncles, friends tried and true.

Couples come to me because they want a ceremony that evades the clichés and that is personalized. More times than not, they're uncertain as to what kind of ceremony they can have if they have no religious backgrounds or if they don't want to incorporate the religious traditions of their families.

So, what can they do?

Here's the thing – the true emotional impact of a ceremony is created by the "visuals." The truest way to personalize your ceremony is to incorporate the people, the significant loves, who are part of the fabric of your life together. This was brought home when I officiated the wedding of Natalie and Mike (names changed).

Mike's family is staunch mid-West Catholic and Natalie's is culturally Jewish. They didn't want a religious ceremony and, in fact, Natalie didn't want "God" mentioned. They did want a ceremony that had a rich texture to it. Here's a snapshot of what we created:

Mike's parents escorted him down the aisle; Natalie's parents escorted her.

They had one reading that was offered by both fathers – and, yes, the dads failed to choke back tears!

After my "words of good cheer" I invited both sets of parents to come up and light the tapers on either side of the Unity Candle that was set inside a protective hurricane lamp. The lamp was on a festive table underneath a Chuppah (the Jewish side was happy to see the Chuppah and the non-Jewish side thought it was a lovely decoration). After the parents lit the tapers, they all hugged Natalie and Mike and returned to their seats. Then Mike and Natalie lit the Unity Candle.

All of this was as a prelude – a moment of blessing by the families – to the Exchange of Vows. In the light of that blessing, Natalie and Mike exchanged their vows. They had written down in booklets their own vows. I invited one of Natalie's grandfathers and one of Mike's grandmothers to present the booklets to them.

The rings were presented by two other grandparents, each of whom has been married for sixty years to their respective spouse, which means the rings were presented from a combined legacy of one hundred and twenty years of married love!

After I pronounced them husband and wife, Mike broke the glass (something he suggested).

While this might sound like a lot of choreography, it actually wasn't. The entire ceremony, from the time I took my place until they kissed, was no more than thirty minutes – and they had a combined total of sixteen attendants (mixed sex on both sides)!

The ceremony was personal because Mike and Natalie incorporated elements that made sense to who they are as a couple and they decided to place the emphasis on family. It was warm and gracious as it honored the sacredness of what they were doing, yet, was not "religious."

20 Easy-to-Forget Things You Need To Remember
As You Prep For Your First Ceremony!

There's much that goes in to making a ceremony not only personal but effective. Just because you know the couple does not mean that the ceremony has now automatically become personalized. You now have to create and script that ceremony.

1. Officiating a ceremony is an honor and a responsibility – treat it as such. Be willing to commit to the time needed to write and practice.

2. There are many styles of officiating. Think back to ceremonies you've attended. What have you liked? Not liked?

3. Be prepared to listen to what the couple says and doesn't say in terms of what they want for their ceremony AND what they want from you. Couples seldom have a clear sense of how they want their ceremony to flow and feel – especially when it's taking place outside a church setting. Part of your job is to help them gain clarity.

4. You are not doing them a "favor" by agreeing to officiate their ceremony. You're giving them the gift of a memory that will last a lifetime.

5. You are a couple's rock, anchor and guide because they will be in an altered state of mind on their wedding day. People will be looking to you for centering and guidance.

6. Your words are the first words of the celebration – you set the tone – and for that reason, make sure you can be heard. Remember to do a mic check. Become familiar with the choreography of the mic and stand. Decide ahead of time if you will hold the mic when they say their vows, or point the mic on a stand in their direction or have them hold the mic. A lapel mic is not always reliable and the bride will never be heard, no matter how awkwardly close you lean in to her.

7. Don't lecture the couple and guests on "what is marriage" – you are there to represent all the guests. You are the voice for the hopes and wishes that are in their hearts. If anyone present doesn't know what marriage is, they're not going to learn it from you within the span of twenty minutes!

8. Everything that happens in a ceremony is playing out on an emotional level. Therefore, you must connect with your own emotions, with the emotions of the guests and with the emotions of the couple. A ceremony falls flat when there's no emotional connection.

9. There is a difference between a ceremony with twenty guests and one with two hundred guests. You have to play to the energy of the crowd in terms of how you speak and use non-verbals.

10. People don't know what to expect so they are concerned. It is a swirl of sights, sounds and emotions. You need to be sure that key players in the ceremony, i.e. readers, musicians, photographer, videographer all know their cues.

11. Keep it real. The couple wants YOU (at your best) to guide them through the ceremony – not you imitating some kind of officiant you think they want.

12. Remember an image, a moment, an incident when you knew they were a couple for keeps. What is a wish you have for them that flows from that memory? Let that memory and that wish be your North Star, your guide, as you prep.

13. Be so prepared that it's like you're simply talking with the couple and their guests and not talking at them. You can never be too prepared.

14. Trust in your script because it is what will allow you to guide the couple and their guests from beginning to end. Don't start to improvise (unless there is a mishap of some kind).

15. A ceremony is a huge balancing act because you've got to be mindful of the couple, their parental units, their relatives, along with friends of the parents, friends of the couple and possible cultural issues and potential religious concerns. The more aware you are, the more you will be able to tailor your words to your audience.

16. Find ways to involve guests because they are the real witnesses. A wedding always takes place within the context of a community – even when a couple elopes.

17. Couples can and do make last minute changes so you need to be quick on your feet. You need to keep your wits about you AND your sense of humor.

18. Dress so that you compliment and do not clash with the couple.

19. The safety of the marriage license is your utmost concern. I can't stress this enough!

20. THE most important thing to remember: a ceremony is not a "thing." It is an experience of people. Be generous and give them your ALL!

There is joy in realizing that you have been part of something bigger than you! That you have been able to give shape and sense to something so profound and so emotional, in a way that engages and refreshes, is an experience unlike anything else.

NEW BONUS #20

Notes For Ceremony Of Same-Sex Couple

In casual conversation and pop culture, people will use the term "gay weddings." I actually don't think there is such a thing as a "gay wedding" – because **a wedding is a wedding!** The ceremony ideas outlined in this book apply equally to the ceremony of a same-sex couple as of a straight couple.

However, there are moments in the ceremony where a same sex couple will have specific options to consider.

Processional and Presentation: Questions to consider include, who will process first? Will each person be escorted by their parents or walk alone? Will they walk down the aisle together?

For the ceremony of my friends Ray and Mike, they were each escorted down the aisle by their parents. When all were at the first row, I asked, "Who presents these men in marriage?" Both sets of parents responded, "We Do!"

I had another couple whose parents were deceased and so each walked down the aisle accompanied by each of their two dogs!

Note: It is always all about being playful and poignant.

Exchange Of Vows and Rings: Your couple decides who will offer their vows first. I suggest that whoever gifts their vows second is the person who offers the ring first. You want to strive to maintain balance throughout the ceremony.

Pronouncement Of Marriage: My experience is that couples vary in how they want to be pronounced and presented. Marc was taking Jose's last name and they wanted the wording to be "Mr. & Mr. Jose and Marc Chavez." Steven and John were not changing last names and did not like the word "husband" as they preferred "spouse." They wanted me to simply pronounce them married and then say, "Now you may kiss" without a "Mr. & Mr." introduction.

Note: The Pronouncement is the culmination of the ceremony and the words used must reflect the preference of the couple.

COACHING SERVICES

As you work through this handbook organizing and writing your ceremony, you may find that you have questions and worries. To help smooth out and punch up your ceremony, I offer affordable coaching either in person or via phone/Skype.

In the process of coaching, I will:

- Review thoroughly your ceremony with you
- Show you how and where to make it even more personal
- Show how to pump up both the sentiment and energy
- Guide you in including everything the couple wants

In addition, I'll coach you how to speak with a confidence that comes from knowing what you're doing.

Please email me at jp@ceremonymadesimple.com so we can discuss how I can help you deliver the memorable ceremony your couple has entrusted to you!

Other Ceremony Resources from JP Reynolds

BOOKS

How To Keep The 'I' In 'I Do'

Is written for couples overwhelmed with the demands of planning their wedding. It's based in the belief that clear, honest, healthy communication goes a long way to reducing stress by cutting through misunderstanding and misperception.

Through the examples of real life wedding stories, I offer couples simple, easy to use communication tips and techniques to help them get heard and understood, with each other, with family members and with vendors. These strategies allow a couple to stay sane by replacing mind games with effective tools for bringing their wedding dream to reality!

Ever Thine, Ever Mine, Ever Ours:
Finding the Words For Your Vows

Is an invitation to slow down and look into your heart as you prepare to offer vows to your partner. I explain the four options for composing your vows and offer basic tips on how to actually say your vows.

Bonus Chapters offer samplings of traditional vows as well as words for exchanging rings. In addition, I help you reflect on what it is you want to say to your partner in your personal vows or in a letter you might exchange with each other on your wedding day.

Both available on Amazon!

Podcast For Wedding Officiants

To learn more about all things ceremony, I invite you to check out my weekly podcast with my colleague Rev. Clint Hufft. Each week we talk about our most recent wedding experiences and adventures!

WeddingCeremonyPodcast.com

For more resources and ideas on how to create YOUR ceremony please visit ~

Ceremonymadesimple.com

ABOUT JP REYNOLDS

Ordained a Catholic priest, JP Reynolds today works as a non-denominational wedding officiant. During the last twenty years, he has celebrated over 1000 weddings – non-denominational, inter-faith, cross-cultural, same-sex. He has created wedding ceremonies that honor the cultural sensitivities of couples that are as spiritually diverse as Muslim/Hindu and Buddhist/Jewish.

His wedding ceremonies have been seen on Lifetime, The Style Network, VH-1, E! Entertainment and The WE where he appeared on Bridezillas. In 2005 he officiated the wedding of Rob and Amber, reality show sweethearts from *Survivor* and *The Amazing Race*.

JP has collaborated with some of the industry's top event planners and is Brides Magazine preferred officiant for their annual Brides Live Wedding Event.

In addition to his responsibilities as a wedding officiant, JP is an executive coach and founder of **The Business of Confidence** (thebusinessofconfidence.com). He coaches people how to present themselves with insight and confidence. His clients range from the not-for-profit sector to the Fortune 500.

JP regularly lectures on issues of business communication and relationships at UCLA Extension and blogs with HuffPo.

JP can be reached with your questions and comments at:

JP@CeremonyMadeSimple.com

Cover Photo: Victor Sizemore   vcsphoto.com